Great Lakes GREAT QUILTS

Includes 12 Projects Celebrating Quilting Traditions

The Great Lakes Quilt Center
Michigan State University Museum

Marsha MacDowell, editor

With contributions from Kitty Clark Cole, Beth Donaldson,
Kate Edgar, Lynne Swanson, and Mary Worrall

Acknowledgments

©2001 by Michigan State University Board of Trustees

Editor: Marsha MacDowell

Developmental Editor: Barbara Konzak Kuhn

Technical Editor: Carolyn Aune

Copy Editors: Carol Barrett and Stacy Chamness

Illustrator and Production Assistant: Jeff Carrillo

Cover and Book Designer: Kristen Yenche

Library of Congress Cataloging-in-Publication Data
Great Lakes, great quilts : 12 projects celebrating
quilt traditions / the Great Lakes Quilt Center, Michigan State
University Museum ; Marsha
MacDowell, editor ; with contributions from Kitty Clark Cole ...
[et al.].
     p. cm.
Includes bibliographical references and index.
  ISBN 1-57120-163-7 (paper trade)
  1. Patchwork--Patterns. 2. Quilting--Patterns. 3. Quilts--
Great Lakes Region--History. 4. Quiltmakers--Great Lakes
Region--Biography.
  I. MacDowell, Marsha. II. Great Lakes Quilt Center.
  TT835 .G334 2001
  746.46'0977--dc21
                              2001002460

Published by C&T Publishing, Inc.
P.O. Box 1456
Lafayette, California 94549

Printed in China
10 9 8 7 6 5 4 3 2 1

Great Lakes, Great Quilts represents the contributions of many in its creation. First to be thanked are Michigan State University Museum development board members Anita Covert and Kitty Clark Cole who have provided financial support and opened up doors to unique partnerships related to the Great Lakes Quilt Center. Wonderful colleagues at the museum share the passion of developing the museum's collection and engaging others in research and education activities related to quilts; they enthusiastically embraced this publication project and toiled hard on the tight deadline. Beth Donaldson, Mary Worrall, Lynne Swanson, Kate Edgar, and Pearl Wong, with the assistance of Francie Freese and Jill Crane, made this truly a team effort. Countless volunteers—both quilters and quilt lovers—have long been instrumental in building the collections and in carrying out the museum's quilt-related activities; their assistance again made this publication possible. Lastly, the museum is grateful to the ongoing generosity of collectors—especially Betty Quarton Hoard, Merry and Albert Silber, Harriet Clarke, and Kitty Clark Cole—who have donated numerous important quilts, and to Eve Boicourt for her donation of a library of almost one thousand quilt-related titles. *Marsha MacDowell*

Individuals wishing to provide financial support, donate quilts or quilt-related ephemera, hold a community Quilt Discovery Day, register their quilt in the Michigan Quilt Project, find out about scheduled exhibits or quilt programs, participate in a collection tour, use the quilt archives or library, contribute to the Michigan Quilt Project Endowment Fund, assist in interviewing quilters, or volunteer in the collections or at the quilt programs at the Great Lakes Folk Festival, can contact the Great Lakes Quilt Center via phone (Quilt Line: 517/432-3800), e-mail (quilts@museum.cl.msu.edu), or mail (Great Lakes Quilt Center, Michigan State University Museum, Michigan State University, East Lansing, Michigan 48824-1045). Additional information can be found at the website: museum@museum.msu.edu.

This activity is part of the Michigan Traditional Arts Program (MTAP) at the Michigan State University Museum which promotes awareness, appreciation, and support for Michigan's traditional cultural resources through research, education, and public service. Operational support for MTAP is provided in part by Michigan State University, the Michigan Council for Arts and Cultural Affairs, and the Michigan State University Extension Service.

Contents

Great Lakes: Quilting and A Sense of Place

THE MICHIGAN STATE UNIVERSITY MUSEUM houses its collection in state-of-the-art cabinets. Quilts are rolled on acid-free tubes and tissue, wrapped with a dust cover of transparent, inert plastic, then placed in roll-out drawers.
Photo by Mary Whalen.

Marsha MacDowell

Wherever quiltmaking occurs in the world, its history and traditions are inevitably tied to a sense of place. To understand quilting in a region, it is helpful to first understand the unique features that help create that sense of place. In the Great Lakes region, a sense of place is dominated, first and foremost, by a physical feature—the Great Lakes themselves. Linked together, these vast, fresh-water bodies form a great inland passageway that has both facilitated and impacted transportation, commerce, and settlement patterns since the first migrations of native peoples into this region.

In the Great Lakes region, tens of thousands of individuals are connected to quilting in one way or another—as artists, teachers, collectors, quilters, quilt teachers, quilt owners, or quilt scholars. Hundreds of exhibitions of quilts have occurred at schools, state and county fairs, powwows, art galleries, and at landmark events such as the World's Columbian Exposition in 1893 in Chicago.

Some exhibitions, like those once hosted by *The Detroit News* at the National Guard Armory in Detroit, those organized by Merry Silber and Sandra Mitchell at the Somerset Mall in Troy, The Sears National Quilt Contest at the 1933 World's Fair in Chicago, and the Quilt Nationals held at the Dairy Barn Southeastern Ohio Cultural Arts Center have been instrumental in raising the awareness of thousands of individuals in quilting.

MEMBERS OF THE RAINY MOUNTAIN KIOWA INDIAN BAPTIST CHURCH in Oklahoma demonstrate quilting while Marsha MacDowell, Curator of Folk Arts, and C. Kurt Dewhurst, Museum Director, look on.
Photo by Mary Whalen.

OCEAN WAVES QUILT

Made by unknown member of the Murphy or Bryant family
c. 1880-1920
Calumet, Houghton County, Michigan
Wool with wool filling
79" x 81"
MSUM 5968.1, Gift of Dorothy Murphy
Photo by KEVA

According to the donor, both this quilt and one similar to it were made by her husband's relatives who hailed from Cornwall, England. The mining industry in Michigan's Upper Peninsula brought many Cornish workers who are also credited with bringing with them the tradition of making pasties, now a fixture of Michigan's cuisine. Heavy, wool, tied quilts with wool filling were typical of those made in or brought to this northern region.

Two individuals—Marie Webster of Marian, Indiana and Mary Schafer of Flushing, Michigan—are known nationally for their pioneering efforts in collecting quilt history. Other individuals such as David Pottinger, Merry and Albert J. Silber, Kitty Clark Cole, Barbara Bannister, Sandra Mitchell, Anita Covert, and Mary McElwain, to name but a few, have been instrumental in forming collections or initiating businesses that have contributed to local, regional, and national quilting and quilt preservation.

Individuals and organizations engage in quilt history documentation efforts and quilt inventories on statewide and local levels in Illinois, Ohio, Wisconsin, Indiana, Michigan, Minnesota, and Ontario. These efforts have yielded important collections of data as well as exhibitions and publications.

The region hosts the Quilter's Hall of Fame in Marian, Indiana and outstanding collections of quilts in both private hands and in such public holdings as the Illinois State Museum, Henry Ford Museum, and the Great Lakes Quilt Center, Michigan State University Museum.

The history and practice of quilting in the Great Lakes region clearly reflects the region's diversity of peoples, resources, and activities. In their patterns, designs, and in related traditions and stories, quilts reflect not only the landscape but also the lives of their makers, their families, and their communities.

PHOTO COLLAGE of scenes from *The Detroit News* Quilt Show, published in *The Detroit News*, November 26, 1933.

The Great Lakes Quilt Center and MSU Museum

LOIS DARCUS and her husband James.
Photo courtesy of Mr. And Mrs. Clarence Husted

The Michigan Quilt Project, begun at the museum in 1984, not only spearheaded the documentation of the state's quilting history, but also stimulated interest in strengthening the museum's quilt collection, upgrading its care, and expanding its use.

Marsha MacDowell

The Michigan State University Museum, founded in 1857, is one of the oldest museums in the Midwest and is accredited by the American Association of Museums. As Michigan's land-grant university museum, it is committed to understanding, interpreting, and respecting natural and cultural diversity. This commitment to society is met through education, exhibitions, research, and the building and stewardship of collections that focus on Michigan and its relationship to the Great Lakes and the world beyond. The museum is a public steward for 2.5 million objects or specimens of cultural and natural history from around the world.

In 1999, the MSU Museum was one of the lead organizations instrumental in founding the Center for Great Lakes Culture whose mission is to "identify, collect, study, interpret, and disseminate the cultural history and expressions of the diverse peoples of the Great Lakes region."

The Michigan Traditional Arts Program is regularly cited as one of the best in the nation. The Michigan Traditional Arts Research Collection of objects, taped interviews, field notes, and photographs relating to folklife provides the only major state resource on this subject and includes materials from all of the surrounding states and provinces.

The Great Lakes Quilt Center has evolved from the sustained and significant quilt-related activities and resources at Michigan State University Museum and the museum's long-standing interest in and commitment to preserving and presenting traditional arts history.

In 2001 the museum and the Great Lakes Quilt Center became formally affiliated with The Alliance for American Quilts as a Regional Center for The Quilt. The Alliance is a national organization established "to further the recognition of quilts; to preserve the history of quilts and quiltmakers; and to establish The Center for The Quilt, a place that actively communicates with people about quilts and quilting."

The primary goals of the center are to record oral and written history documenting quilting and the personal histories of quiltmakers, expand and maintain a research collection of information on Great Lakes quilting, initiate educational and exhibition programs to bring quilting history to a wider audience, increase awareness of textile conservation issues and support preservation efforts of endangered textiles, identify and recognize quilters and quilting traditions from diverse regional, social, economic, and ethnic backgrounds, honor outstanding individual quilters and quilt groups, and publish information on Great Lakes quilts, quilters, and quilting.

CRAZY QUILT

Roe G. Van Deusen, designer;
Lois Van Deusen Darcus
(1865-1926), piecer
Designed 1885-1887, pieced
and finished 1887
Elsie, Clinton County, Michigan
Velvet and silk
65" x 74"
MSUM 7097.1; Gift of Mr.
and Mrs. Clarence Husted
Photo © Peter Glendinning

According to family history,
the quilt was made by teenager
Lois Van Deusen for her
father, Roe G. Van Deusen,
whose initial is in the lower
left-hand corner. Roe
designed the stitches, which
he drew in a notebook entitled
"Fancy Stitches for Crazy
Work" and asked Lois to
duplicate in embroidery form.

TILE (or Puzzle)
Summer Spread

Made by an unidentified
ladies' group
Dated in the applique 1872
Paw Paw, Van Buren County,
Michigan
Cotton
76" x 88"
MSUM 1998:76.1
Photo by Mary Whalen

"Tile" quilts, sometimes also
called "Puzzle" quilts, are
made of randomly-shaped
pieces appliquéd individually
onto a square block of white
foundation fabric. To make
the "tile" effect, a space is left
between each piece as it is
appliquéd onto the background.

A note, dated 1929, which
accompanied this appliquéd
piece as it was handed down
within the family indicated
that the summer spread was
made by a group of ladies
who were 'old timers' and who
all belonged to the same church
in the village of Paw Paw.

RESEARCH

Through fieldwork, archival research, and a series of community Quilt Discovery Days, center staff work with students and volunteers to locate, document, and collect information and materials on quilts and quilters. For special projects, tape-recorded interviews are conducted with quilters in their homes, and quilting activities, such as auctions, exhibits, contests, and bees, are also documented.

The Great Lakes Quilt Save Our Stories project and Michigan Boxes Under the Bed® projects (developed with The Alliance for American Quilts) provide guilds with oral history training and short-term loans of equipment and reference materials to record quilting stories and history in their communities.

With The Alliance for American Quilts and the American Quilt Study Group, the Michigan State University Museum was instrumental in establishing H-QUILTS, a moderated internet discussion forum whose purpose is to provide an exchange of information for individuals around the world engaged in quilting research and documentation. In 2001, the Michigan State University Museum launched H-GREAT LAKES QUILTS for those specifically interested in Great Lakes quilting research and documentation.

NANCY HOWARD interviews Virginia Anderson at the 2000 National Folk Festival "Great Lakes Stories" Stage. Tape-recorded interviews with quilt owners, quilters, and others involved in quilting is an important component of the Great Lakes Quilt Center activities.
Photo by Mary Whalen

AUNT CLEMY'S RIBBON QUILT (Sawtooth Star Quilt)

Maker unknown
c. 1880
Provenance unknown
Silk, glass beads, paper labels
30³/₄" x 60"
MSUM 1997:98.1; Gift of
Annette Shaver
Photo by Mary Whalen

Quilts often include scraps of fabrics leftover from making clothing or from used clothing. Stitched to twenty of the fabric pieces in this quilt are tiny paper tags with notes, written in pencil, detailing the source of the fabric. With the use of these sentimental tags and expensive fabrics, this little quilt conjures up images of a close-knit, well-off Victorian family.

TRACY MILLER FAMILY QUILT

Delphine Paulus Miller
(b. ca. 1868-?)
1930-1936
Detroit, Wayne County, Michigan
Cotton with cotton filling
67½" x 81½"
MSUM 6594.1; Gift of Tracy and Joanne Miller
Photo by KEVA

This extraordinary one-of-a-kind quilt, made as a gift for Miller's son Tracy and his wife Margaret, is composed of intricate appliquéd designs taken from her original drawings and her mother's original paper cuts. Miller wrote: [Detroit hasn't] found me out yet, but they're going to. I'll probably have some of my work in the *News* soon, then hope to do something worthwhile "yet" even though I am almost 67. It is never too late to try, even if I have been trying all my life.

Delphine Paulus Miller, second from top, with her sisters, taken in Detroit. Photo courtesy of Tracy and Joanne Miller

PROGRAMS AND PUBLICATIONS

Quilt programs have always been a part of the annual folklife festivals produced by the Michigan State University Museum; the programs include demonstrations of quilting, on-stage discussions of quilting, and hands-on activities for festival visitors. The Festivals of Michigan Folklife (1987-1998) included programs featuring Native American quilting, fundraising quilts, multi-cultural quilting, quilting from the "Thumb" area of Michigan, African-American quilting, family quilts, and the NAMES Project Quilt. For the National Folk Festivals (1999-2001), a special "Great Lakes, Great Quilts" program included opportunities to register quilts in the Michigan Quilt Project Inventory, record quilt stories, learn about quilt care and first aid, as well as demonstrations and discussion of quilting by invited traditional artists. The museum's Great Lakes Folk Festival, to be launched in 2002, will continue the "Great Lakes, Great Quilts" program.

The Collections

In 1952, the first quilts were accessioned into the MSU Museum's collections when the museum acquired the entire contents of the another museum which was dismantled. Built primarily through donations from collectors and quilters and augmented by a small acquisition fund, the museum quilt collection now numbers more than 450 significant historical and contemporary quilts.

Unique collections include The Mary Schafer Quilt and Ephemera Collection, The Kitty Clark Cole Collection, The Merry and Albert J. Silber Collection, The Clarke Family Quilt Collection, The Durkee-Blakeslee-Quarton-Hoard Family Quilt Collection, The Michigan African-American Quilt Collection, and The North American Indian and Native Hawaiian Quilt Collection.

The Great Lakes Quilt Center also houses the Michigan Quilt Project files and the collections of materials (tape-recorded interviews, photos, field notes, patterns and other ephemera) generated by the center's research projects. In addition, the center includes a room-use only library of over 1000 quilt and textile titles, including the Eve Boicourt collection.

By the close of the 20th century, the museum's quilt-related research, collection, and education activities have grown substantially and are now recognized nationally. Through the dedicated energy and support of many individuals and organizations the center has become an important agent in the preservation of quilts and quilt ephemera as well as a leader in the development of innovative programs to make the collections and resources widely available for educational and research use.

PICTORIAL BLOCK QUILT

Catharine Weber (b. 1874, d. ?)
1914
Morenci, Lenawee County, Michigan
Cotton, velvet, felt and wool, embroidery thread
62½" x 65"
MSUM 1999:11.1
Photo by Mary Whalen

Each of the nine panels in this quilt block is framed with crazy quilt-style embroidery stitches and features a scene or inscription embellished with a combination of appliquéd fabrics and embroidery stitches. The cross-stitched inscriptions read "Catharine Weber, Morenci, 1914, Age 40" and "to Louise F. Borton, March 9, 1914." The clothing on the figures reflects that of the quilt's era.

AN ORNITHOLOGICAL QUILT (PICTORIAL BLOCKS)

Chloe A. Barnum Kimball
(1822-1873)
1869
Bennington, Shiawassee
County, Michigan
Cotton
74" x 79"
MSUM 7595.2
Photo by KEVA

Chloe Kimball was born in Pompey, New York and came to Michigan with her family sometime before 1853, when she married Martin C. Kimball, by whom she had two daughters. Fond of nature, she made at least two other quilts containing birds and flowers. This quilt passed first to Kimball's daughter, Leora Kimball Rinehard, and then to her great-granddaughter, Kathleen Common Schmidt.

CRAZY PINWHEEL QUILT

Edna Freshour
1860-1870
Hillsdale, Michigan
Cotton and silk
70" x 72"
MSUM 6616.1;
Gift of William R. Freshour
Photo by KEVA

Only two facts about this quilt have been documented. Edna Freshour was a resident of Hillsdale County, Michigan, when she made this quilt, and she used scraps of silk lining material from a women's high-button shoe factory to construct the 16 large blocks. The use of a variety of shapes and colors throughout the blocks gives the impression that the pinwheels are in motion.

North American Indian and Native Hawaiian Quilt Collection

Today the Hawaiian flag quilt continues to have meaning for many Native Hawaiians. Sharon Balai, will not make one that is bed-sized because she does not want it used on a bed. "I don't think people should sit on the [flag] quilt. It's like a desecration to our honor, you know, our background, our ancestry. I wouldn't sit on anybody's flag. Each flag represents that special group of people and although we cannot agree on everything in the world, we can agree to respect you for being who you are."

Marsha MacDowell

Native quilters in the Hawaiian Islands and on the North American continent have long used colors and designs distinctly their own to make quilts which function in ways both similar to other cultural groups as well as in ways that have specific tribal or pan-Indian meanings.

Quilts have been used in nearly every Native community for everyday purposes. In some communities, quilts are also used to honor individuals, in ceremonies, and in a variety of activities that strengthen community life.

Native peoples in the Hawaiian Islands and North America have always had many indigenous traditions of textile production and use; the materials and skills of quiltmaking had many precedents in these communities. When commercially-manufactured cloth and steel needles became available to native peoples, it was not surprising that, adept at similar craft forms, they quickly picked up quiltmaking.

Native needleworkers continually combine or replace old materials and technologies with new. Finger-woven animal pelt blankets have been replaced by wool blankets and quilts, hides replaced by cotton fabrics, and awls and needles replaced by sewing machines and rotary cutters.

The initial conveyance of quilting skills to Native peoples occurred in the nineteenth century with the establishment of mission schools and churches in Native communities.

Whether Mennonite missions on Hopi land, Mormon missions in Utah and Nevada, Quaker mission schools in Pennsylvania, or Catholic missions in frontier outposts, Christian evangelical and educational efforts were instrumental in introducing and sustaining interest in these crafts.

Within Native communities, quilts are often used to mark rites of passage or special occasions and to honor individuals for their special achievements or contributions. At naming ceremonies, quilts are given to friends and family in honor of the loved one being named. Students graduating from high school or college are given quilts as a sign of recognition of their academic accomplishments. Athletes winning competitive events are given quilts for their physical achievements. Veterans returning from military service are honored with quilts to thank them for their bravery and personal sacrifice.

Anyone who has contributed significantly to his or her own, family's, or community's well being is honored, either by being given a quilt or having quilts given away on their behalf.

Production techniques material preparation, patchwork patterns, quilting designs, and quilt names were shared among Native and non-Native quiltmakers.

Choices of patterns, construction techniques, materials, and names often are tied to Native or tribal identity. Native artists adapt the beadwork, rug weaving, and basket weaving patterns of their cultural heritage or of their own experience into their quilts. Color choices often reflect the Native quilter's close spiritual ties to the natural world. Many times Native quilters, irrespective of their own tribal background, will select printed fabrics that incorporate Southwestern or pan-Indian imagery.

There are a number of reasons why Native quilters have been so little known to those outside their families or communities and that museums have so few examples in their collections, but

perhaps the chief reasons were that it is an art form that has appeared so extensively in everyday life and that it was primarily the result of indigenous cultural contact with outsiders.

Of all of the discrete collections of the MSU Museum's quilt collections, perhaps the most important is the collection of North American Indian and Native Hawaiian quilts. No other museum in the world has a collection that not only represents the breadth and diversity of Native quilting in North America but also is accompanied by documentary information resulting from historical and ethnographic research.

Considered commonplace and perceived firmly tied to a European rather than a Native artistic tradition, quilts, unlike other Native arts, were historically not collected or studied as items of ethnographic, aesthetic, or marketplace value.

ETHEL ADAIR at her home.

Photo courtesy of Ruth Steiner, collection of Michigan State University Museum.

A NEW TIME

Nancy Naranjo (Eastern Cherokee)
1996
Frederick, Maryland
82" x 58"
MSUM 1996:96; North American Indian and Native Hawaiian Quilt Collection
Photo by Elbinger Studios, Inc.

By combining painted and dyed fabric with appliquéd and embroidered detailed images, Nancy Naranjo achieves a painterly effect. Embroidered at the bottom is the phrase, "In the early Spring morning, The People begin reuniting from small, wintering groups. Emissaries of Morning Star and White Buffalo Calf Woman come, carrying The Pipe. The time of healing, of coming back together to start a new time, is here." Most of her work is intended as wall-hangings and Naranjo is among a small number of Native quilters who have begun to show their work in galleries and museums.

HAWAIIAN FLAG QUILT

Harriet Soong, quilter
(Native Hawaiian);
Sharon Balai, designer,
(Native Hawaiian)
1997
Waimea and Kailua-Kona,
Hawaii
56" x 54"

MSUM1997:72
Gift of Harriet Soong and
Sharon Balai
Photo by Elbinger Studios, Inc.

The Hawaiian flag was first
designed for King
Kamehameha I prior to 1816.
Expressing their allegiance to
Hawaiian sovereignty,
Hawaiians began making
quilts, named *Ku'u Hae Aloha*
(My Beloved Flag). Balai
and Soong felt strongly that
a flag quilt should be in the
exhibition "To Honor and
Comfort: Native Quilting
Traditions". The motto "Ua
mau ke ea o ka aina i ka
pono" translates in English as
"The life of the land is perpet-
uated in righteousness."

BANDOLIER BAG VARIATION QUILT

Carole Stewart (Muscogee
Creek)
1996
Washington, Oklahoma
88¹/₄" x 82¹/₂"
MSUM1996:106
Photo by Elbinger Studios, Inc.

"Despite the fact Stewart
travels the world as a profes-
sional business woman, she
lives in her native community
and remains firmly tied to it
and its traditions, including
those related to quilting."

J. "Jimmie" Carole Stewart
says that in her tribe, "the
quilt is an important part of
the burial tradition. One of
the last gestures the family is
able to perform for the
deceased is to drape a hand-
made quilt over the coffin
before it is buried."

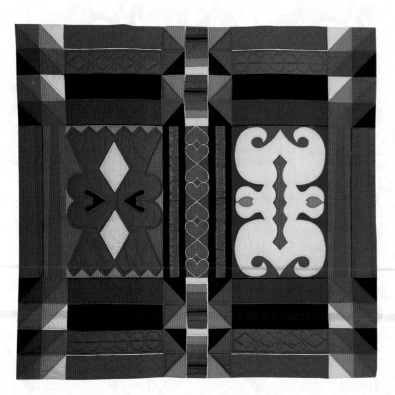

GRAND ENTRY LONE STAR QUILT

Shirley Grady
(Mandan/Hidatsa/Sioux/Crow)
1995
New Town, North Dakota
80" x 93"
MSUM 7603.1
Photo: Elbinger Studios, Inc.

Shirley Grady shares, "My great-grandmothers, all our great-grandmothers and grandmothers made patchwork quilts. It was only in the 1950s that some people brought home some Star quilts from the Sioux ladies . . . and then, all the ones that were sewing in my reservation picked up that Star quilt."

This innovative version of the Star quilt incorporates appliquéd feathers in the corners and a border of pieced Star tips. The quilting includes an elaborate rendition of the invited leaders of a powwow "grand entry" as well as feathers and many other figures. Grady has also incorporated her clan symbol, the wolf, as part of her signature on the quilt.

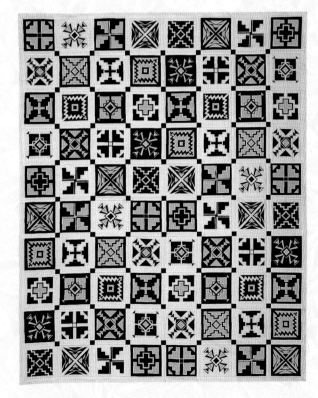

NAVAJO DESIGNS QUILT

Jennifer Tsosie (Navajo)
1996
Flagstaff, Arizona
67½" x 84"
MSUM1996:122
Photo: Elbinger Studios, Inc.

In this one-of-a-kind black and white quilt, Tsosie replicates a different rug design in each block.

Tsosi is also a talented fashion designer whose clothing also incorporates design elements drawn from rugs and other Native American traditional arts.

The Michigan African-American Quilt Collection

The work of more than thirty quilters was recorded at the first event held in Muskegon, and at a Quilt Discovery Day in Detroit, Rosa Parks brought her and her mother's quilts in to be registered.

Marsha MacDowell

Early African-American residents in the Great Lakes region were usually foreign born or from Eastern states, but, by the early-twentieth-century, the majority came from Ohio, Indiana, Kentucky, Tennessee, West Virginia, and Virginia. The last great wave of African-American migration to this region occurred during the period of World War II and the migrants came mainly from the Carolinas and the Deep South states of Mississippi, Georgia, and Alabama.

The Michigan State University Museum's collection of African-American quilts grew out of an effort begun in 1985 to aggressively collect information on African-American quilting history in the state.

Working with local organizations in communities of predominantly black populations or historically important black settlements, museum staff held a series of African-American Community Quilt Discovery Days in 1986. Due to the active involvement of African-American leaders in these communities, the African-American Quilt Discovery Days successfully identified many quilts and quilters.

BLUE JEAN POCKETS QUILT

Essie Lee Robinson (b. 1918)
1990
Detroit, Wayne County, Michigan
Cotton with cotton filling
78" x 90"
MSUM 7536.1
Photo by Mary Whalen

Essie Robinson was known for her creative approaches to quilt design and loved making quilts. She stated, "Quilting [is] a reason to get up in the morning. It works my brain creatively." Dora Gardner, a Michigan quilter who makes quilts from pieces of jeans pants, generally calls quilts from jeans "britches quilts."

The documentation project and the subsequent collection of quilts reveals a wide range of individual styles and traditions of quilting designs, construction techniques, and uses within Michigan's African-American communities. This breadth provided an opportunity to examine major controversies in African-American quilt scholarship—the issues of African survivals in African-American material culture and whether or not there exists a "typical" African-American quilt.

Most studies of African-American quilting, or what Cuesta Benberry refers to as "ethnic quilting," have been based on quilts and quilters with strong ties to Southern, rural communities, the areas of the country where the majority of the African slave populations originally existed and where their descendants still live. It is not surprising then, that so many quilts containing the characteristics of African textiles are found in this region. The Michigan data included "typical African-American" quilts, generally made by women who had been born and raised in the South and who migrated north and/or who kept in close contact with relatives who lived in the South. However, research also documented quilts reflecting many other traditions rooted in a variety of other experiences, including urban, Northern, multi-ethnic, occupational, and African. Thus the collection does not reflect a "typical African-American" quilt type, but a diversity of styles, pattern names, techniques, and uses found within the Michigan African-American experience.

CROW FOOT IN THE MUD QUILT

Sina Phillips (b. 1901, died unknown year)
1983
Muskegon, Muskegon County, Michigan
Collection of Michigan State University Museum.
Cotton and polyester
72" x 80"
MSUM 6788.1
Photo by KEVA

Sina Phillips learned the art of "making covers" from her mother, Ida Jones, at the age of ten. In Alabama, Phillips participated in numerous quilting bees, "we had a regular quiltin' bee at home in the wintertime, you know, that's all we had to do. After we got through farmin' we'd go from house to house and quilt."

Sina Phillips's contention that "any colors look good together" is proven in this quilt top that she calls *Crow Foot in the Mud*.

STRING QUILT

Rosie L. Wilkins (b. 1911, died unknown year)
1980s
Muskegon, Muskegon County, Michigan
Satin with polyester filling
62" x 83"
MSUM 2000:72
Photo by Mary Whalen

Rosie Wilkins first learned to quilt from her mother. Wilkins figured she made over 100 quilts in her lifetime and quilting was a part of her daily routine.

One of the rare times Wilkins bought a pattern was when she was twelve or fourteen years old. Her family attended a touring entertainment show which featured a girl who did paper cuts with her feet. Wilkins made several quilts from the unique pattern she purchased from that girl.

Rosie Wilkins
Photo by Bruce Fox

The International Textile Collection

back of Appliqué Quilt

APPLIQUÉ QUILT

Maker unknown (Chinese)
c.1996
Badaling region, China
Cotton, cotton/polyester, silk,
denim, velvet
54" x 65"
MSUM 1996.86.1; Gift of Liz
Schweitzer
Photo by Mary Whalen

Contemporary visitors to the
Great Wall in the Badaling
region outside of Beijing,
China have the opportunity
to purchase a great array of
hand-crafted items including
the "five poisonous creatures"
— toad, snake, centipede,
lizard, scorpion — locally
believed to ward away evil
spirits. This particular piece
was purchased from a woman
walking and carrying her
wares on top of the wall.

Marsha MacDowell

Throughout history, piecing, appliquéing, and quilting techniques have been employed by individuals to construct and decorate textiles for both ceremonial and everyday uses. Michigan State University Museum's collections hold many historical and contemporary examples of textiles that incorporate these techniques. The MSUM holds a collection of over 100 Nigerian *kente* cloths, composed of pieced-together woven strips. Other examples include Peruvian *cuadros* (pictorial appliquéd scenes depicting political and labor struggles), Indian pieced cotton patchwork pillow covers (often embellished with mirrors and using star and block designs), intricately cut and reverse-appliquéd Panamanian *molas*, and a set of nineteenth-century Egyptian ceremonial tent panels that are appliquéd and decorated with calligraphic inscriptions.

Over the past twenty years special attention has been given to expanding the textile collection so that comparisons can be made between work produced in the Great Lakes region and other patchwork and appliqué traditions around the world.

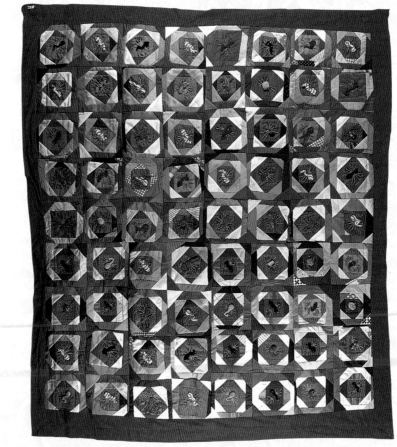

ZINNIA VARIATION QUILT

Leona Johnson (Liberian),
b. 1944
1992
Monrovia, Liberia, Africa
Cotton, polyester batting
94" x 96"
MSUM 7435.2
Photo by Mary Whalen

Modern-day Liberia was founded in the early 1800s largely by freed slaves from the United States and records listed seamstresses among some of the earliest settlers.

Though the history of quilting in Liberia has been traced to the nineteenth century, self-help quilting cooperatives established in the last quarter of the 20th century have quickly grown in membership and productivity.

PAJ NTAUB

Poi Xiong (Hmong)
c. 1985
Detroit, Michigan
Cotton/polyester
24" x 24"
MSUM 2000:72.2
Photo by Philip C. Brautigan

Paj ntaub (literally "flower cloth") is the appliquéd and embroidered textile work traditionally made by Hmong women for their clothing.

This piece, collected in Lansing, Michigan from the artist, incorporates a very traditional embroidered Hmong design in the central square set within an American quilt appliqué-style block pattern.

"SARAI MUGARE" WEYA CLOTH

Attributed to Robert
Magurambe (Weya man)
1999-2000
Harare area, Zimbabwe
Cotton
23" x 35"
MSUM 2000:30.1; G
Photo by Mary Whalen

"Weya" cloth refers to a
distinctive style of appliquéd
pictorial textiles done by
women in the Weya, a rural
area in Zimbabwe. Artists
chose stories or themes that
reflect their experiences,
beliefs, and attitudes.

Though Weya appliqués are
traditionally done by Weya
women in Zimbabwe, this
piece was attributed in
Harare to a Weya man.

This piece tells the sad story
of a woman who hung herself
after her husband beat her
and left her for a second wife.

SAMPLER QUILT

Rafiu Aderemi Mustapha
(Nigerian), b. February 2, 1973
December 1998
Santa Fe, New Mexico
Cotton
90" x 93"
MSUM 2000:66.1
Photo by Mary Whalen

The Niké Center for Arts and
Culture was established in
1988 in Osogbo, Nigeria by
Niké Olaniyi Davies-Okundaye.

Shortly after the center
opened, Georgina Beier, a
European, taught members
how to make quilts out of
their cloth and found that the
men were more enthusiastic
than women about this new
art form. Yoruba artist Rafiu
"Remi" Mustapha, "My quilt
is trying to talk about unity
in Africa as a whole with
the way I used the different
colors of fabric."

Family Quilt Collections

Lynne Swanson and Mary Worrall

The relationship of family structures and quilting history has long been firmly entwined. For many individuals, it is within a family context that the first quilting stitches are learned, the first quilting stories shared, and the first quilts made, given, received, and used. Shared quilting activities often serve as an important means of strengthening family bonds.

Family history is often embedded, sometimes purposefully and sometimes by accident, within a quilt. Many quilts are made to mark family celebrations or rites of passage such as births, naming ceremonies, graduations, marriages, anniversaries, and deaths. Memories of family activities and traditions can be communicated through pictorial depictions and literal inscriptions as well as the use of fabrics worn by family members. When handed down from one generation to the next, a quilt is a tangible reminder (sometimes the only existing one) of a forebear, and serves as both a physical and emotional tie to that individual's past.

The collections of the Michigan State University Museum contains many strong examples of quilts that document and convey family history. Of special interest are two large collections of quilts—The Clarke Family Quilt Collection and The Durkee-Blakeslee-Quarton-Hoard Family Quilt Collection—which contain the work of several generations of their respective families.

The Clarke Family Quilt Collection

The Clarke Family Quilt Collection, given to Michigan State University Museum in 1986 by Dr. Harriet A. Clarke and her brother, George M. Clarke, includes forty-five quilts and quilt tops completed between 1926 and 1946 by Bozena Vilhemina Clarke, her daughter Laura May Clarke, and daughter-in-law Emilie Ann Clarke. The collection also includes numerous hand-made templates and patterns, unique hand-colored graphs of planned quilts, newspaper and magazine clippings, and personal inventory notes written by the quilters.

The collection also provides an excellent study example for understanding quilting activity in Detroit during this period and the relationship of the Clarke family quilters to the regional and national rejuvenation of interest in quiltmaking and home arts of the 1920s to the 1940s.

It is generally known that quilting and domestic arts enjoyed a resurgence of activity, acceptance, and popularity during the Great Depression and the 1940s.

With the resurgence of interest in quilting, many new pattern and fabric companies came into being to take advantage of the new market of consumers eager to join the fad of producing and decorating their homes with quilts.

Though the patterns were often based on traditional patterns, one can see a distinct shift in the look of quilts from this period. Designers chose to use a new palette of clear, solid pastel colors, and small-figured print fabrics, newly available through advances in the textile industry. They favored appliqué patterns with a central medallion, often in a floral motif. The resulting quilts are homogeneous in style and palette and clearly indicative of the period.

The Clarke collection is a textbook collection of these "Depression Era" style quilts. Because the quilts in the collection were largely unused, they are in excellent condition; the lovely pastel colors and figurative prints popular during the Depression era are still bright and vivid.

The Clarke family quilts had been carefully stored through the years by Dr. Harriet Clarke, granddaughter of Bozena V. Clarke. Dr. Clarke greatly valued the collection of quilts, patterns, templates, and paper materials as documents of her own family's history and creative process.

Of her donation Dr. Clarke says:

Quilts are very lovely things and it [the quilt project] made me feel like I didn't want her family quilts to be distributed here and there...I couldn't bear to part with them myself. I didn't want to sell them or anything like that and...I felt so good about having all those quilts stay together, that they wouldn't get separated and washed and become unknown,...that there was a lot of diligent and loving work that went into them, and that they are family treasures.

ROSE WREATH QUILT

Bozena V. Clarke (b. 1871)
1935-1937
Detroit, Wayne County, Michigan
Cotton
76¾" x 91¾"
MSUM 6119.35; Gift of Dr. Harriet A. Clarke and George M. Clarke
Photo by Mark Eifert

Bozena Vilhemina Clarke was a tailor before her marriage in 1896. At the age of 50, she learned to quilt from members of the Rebecca Jane Circle, the quilt group that met at her church. Harriet Clarke remembers some of her grandmother Clarke's quilting activities:

[Her] custom was to piece quilts in the warmer months as these could be carried in a basket or box and taken by car to the family summer cottage. [She] quilted in the winter months usually, after Christmas, about two or three hours each afternoon until spring or until the quilt or quilts. . .were done.

Bozena used 3,028 pieces in the center of this quilt made with an Anne Orr pattern.

TRIP AROUND THE WORLD QUILT

Bozena V. Clarke (b. 1871) and Laura M. Clarke, designers; Laura M. Clarke, piecer; members of the Rebecca Jane Circle, quilters
Made 1932-33
Detroit, Wayne County, Michigan
Cotton
80" x 80"
MSUM: 6119.6; Gift of Harriet and George M. Clarke
Photo by Mark Eifert

When Bozena and Laura saw a quilt similar to this on display at the Hudson's Department Store in downtown Detroit, they immediately began planning to make one themselves. Together they made a detailed, hand-colored diagram, then Laura pieced it, and lastly it was quilted by their quilting group, the Rebecca Jane Circle from the Union Boulevard Congregational Church. RJR Fabrics, Inc. is developing a fabric line which will reproduce every fabric in Clarke's quilt.

Durkee-Blakeslee-Quarton-Hoard Family Quilt Collection

"If you have a cat, you do not use quilts," firmly states Betty Quarton Hoard. Concerned that family pets might damage a collection of pristine family quilts prompted Betty to donate seventeen quilts made by her grandmother, Martha L. Durkee Blakeslee and great-grandmother, Mary Elizabeth Beardslee Durkee to the Michigan State University Museum.

The Durkee-Blakeslee-Quarton-Hoard Collection contains a strong representation of quilt styles and patterns popular during the last third of the nineteenth century. Prominent in the quilts of Mary Durkee are coppery madder prints in browns and dark oranges, chocolates, double pinks, and purples.

Betty's grandfather, Frank Blakeslee, owned a dry-goods store in Birmingham, the city in which Betty continues to reside. Ownership of the store undoubtedly contributed to the eclectic variety of fabric dating to the era that are found throughout the family's quilts. Betty also remembers a quilt frame that, one winter, was set up so frequently in the dining room that the family could not sit around the table to eat.

Betty's own quilting began with a detailed redwork piece created with her sister, Winnie. The project commenced when Betty was about fourteen, an age she thought was too old for this task and thus only completed four of the blocks. Winnie finished the remainder. The motifs embroidered on blocks set with a red sashing include numerous depictions of nursery rhymes and fairy tales. Today, Betty proudly displays the quilt in her home.

Both the Durkee-Blakeslee-Quarton-Hoard and the Clarke collections are valuable because of the good condition in which the families kept the quilts and the related materials that were donated along with the textiles. Preserved now within a museum dedicated to research and education, it is hoped that these material cultural collections will be used not only to understand the lives of Detroit-area families, but also to contribute to many regional, women's, and textile studies.

WREATH OF ROSES QUILT

Mary E. Beardslee Durkee
c. 1860
Franklin, Oakland County,
Michigan
Cotton
74" x 92"
MSUM 1999:12.4; Gift of
Betty Quarton Hoard
Photo by Mary Whalen

The rose was among the most common motifs selected for 19th century appliquéd quilts. Red, yellow, and green fabric appliquéd to a white background grew in popularity as the reliability of dyes increased during the mid-1800s. This quilt, representative of its time period, was created by the donor's great-grandmother.

ALBUM OR SIGNATURE
QUILT (Chimney Sweep or
Christian Cross Quilt)

Mary E. Beardslee Durkee
c. 1860
Oakland County, Michigan
Cotton
80" x 88"
MSUM 1999:12.2; Gift of
Betty Quarton Hoard
Photo by Mary Whalen

Signature quilts are traditionally thought of as a group
project of individuals who
share a link. This particular
quilt, however, is unique in
that every block features sig-
natures with the name "Mary
E. Durkee" or "M. E.
Durkee" applied in the same
stamped design. One can
only wonder if Mary was test-
ing out her new stamps, or
perhaps she was just having a
lot of fun showing off her
own name.

The Clarkes saved everything
associated with their quiltmaking. Pictured here are
a variety of hand-made templates, the hand-colored
design for Trip Around the
World quilt, and an inventory
book listing all the quilts
they produced.
Photo by Mary Whalen.

"ROLLING STONE" QUILT (Bow Tie Quilt)

Martha Durkee Blakeslee
c. 1890
Farmington, Oakland County, Michigan
Cotton
74" x 88"
MSUM 7410.2; Gift of Betty Quarton Hoard
Photo by KEVA

Betty Quarton Hoard remembers the blue plaid fabric used in this quilt, one of her favorites, was also used in other family quilts. Called "Rolling Stone" by the family, this quilt was made with Bow Tie pattern blocks in a Snowball setting. Simple patterns were popular as the 19th century drew to a close and this tied, utilitarian quilt with fabrics in a wide array of colors and styles is representative of the time.

OHIO STAR QUILT

Mary E. Beardslee Durkee
c. 1870
Oakland County, Michigan
Cotton
68" x 77¼"
MSUM 1999.12.3; Gift of Betty Quarton Hoard
Photo by Mary Whalen

The family dry-goods store would have offered the perfect opportunity to collect the printed fabrics found in this Evening Star or Sawtooth Star design, called by family "Ohio Star." Among the most distinctive of the period were madder browns in a variety of stripes and other geometric prints.

Collections By Collectors

Lynne Swanson and Mary Worrall

col·lect (kə-lekt')v. **1.** To bring or gather together in a group: assemble. **2.** To accumulate from a number of sources.

Collectors are often said to be driven by a passion to attain the next perfect or unique object for their collection. This could not be more true for many quilt collectors. Whether seeking examples with the tiniest stitches, dazzling fabrics, original designs, exquisite workmanship, or of historical significance, the quilt collector ultimately pieces together a unique assemblage of works that reflects his or her interests and knowledge.

Michigan State University Museum has been the fortunate recipient of several collections amassed by passionate collectors. These collections provide us with material that help us explore the relationship between objects, their makers, and their users (including the collectors). Three of these collections are featured here.

The Albert and Merry Silber Collection

Merry Silber began her collecting career in the field of fine art prints and thought of quilts simply as bed coverings or furniture moving pads. In the 1970s, however, she saw her daughter Julie Silber's [formerly of Mary Strickler's Quilt Shop, now of Quilt Complex, Inc., Albion, California] walls covered with many fabulous flea market finds. Until that time she "had no idea of the value, beauty, artistry of

American patchwork quilts. . .With the unflagging support of my husband Al, I found a new love and a new career late in life. At the time it was somewhat surprising to me that the transition from my deep involvement with the world of theater, music and art would be so easy, but when you think about it, quilts are indeed dramatic, rhythmical, and painterly!"

The Mary Schafer Quilt Collection

During the period between the quilting revivals of the 1940s and the 1970s, Mary Schafer of Flushing, Michigan emerged as an important quiltmaker, historian, and collector in American quilt studies. At a young age, Mary's interest in needlework was nurtured when women in her neighborhood taught her sewing, tatting, and other needlework forms.

For quilters, inspiration appears in many forms; in 1956 Mary Schafer found hers while cleaning out the trunk of her car. Her son had recently returned from military service, and the homecoming was celebrated with a beach party. Picking up after the event, Mary discovered a wet and dirty unclaimed quilt that had been used as a beach blanket. Wanting to honor the quiltmaker, Mary washed and repaired the quilt in attempt to restore the piece to its glory days. She then created a classic red and white reproduction featuring an original border and quilting designs—elements that became Mary's trademarks. This was Mary's first pieced quilt.

Merry and Albert J. Silber.

In her collecting, Merry looks for works that attract her, and she is drawn to the "design, color, artistry, and originality of these wonderful artists who put together wonderful designs out of scraps of fabrics.

Mary Schafer in her home.

Kitty Clark Cole holds a quilt made by her great-grand-mother Mary Jane "Bird" Jamison Clark. Behind Kitty is a quilt pieced by Shirley Shenk of Goshen, Indiana and quilted by a group of Amish women from Goshen. The quilt was the first quilt Kitty purchased.
Photo by Pearl Yee Wong

Many of Kitty's family members have served in the military and Kitty feels that collecting quilts with patriotic motifs is a reflection of her heritage.

The donation of these quilts and her generosity in supporting collection care, education, and research have strengthened the collection immeasurably.

As Mary researched to find the name of the pattern, she became a subscriber to *Aunt Kate's Quilting Bee* and began to amass every reference to quilting she could find. Unable to find the pattern's name and because the design reminded her of a mill wheel, Mary named it "Linden Mill" after the only nationally registered historical site in her home of Genessee County at the time.

Mary was growing increasingly more interested in quilt history. In order to learn more she began to collect quilts, quilt tops, and vintage fabric which she often incorporated into a new top. Mary transformed many, many old tops into finished quilts and would often design original border, create a unique quilting design, and have the top finished by someone else.

One of Mary's strongest friendships to grow out of the round robin exchanges was with Betty Harriman of Bunceton, Missouri who was introduced to Mary through Barbara Bannister, a mutual friend. Mary and Betty shared many of the same tastes in quilt patterns as well as an interest in history. They never met in person but their friendship flourished first through an exchange of letters and later through regular telephone conversations. The pair frequently would work on the same design, each creating their own inter-pretation of a pattern. Following Betty's death in 1971, Mary purchased Betty's unfinished quilts from the family. Bringing Betty's projects to completion continued Mary's tie to her friend.

By the time the quilting revival of the 1970s emerged, Mary Schafer had become a well-known figure in the quilting world. Within the Great Lakes region she spoke to many groups on both historical and technical aspects of quilting. She participated in contests and quilt shows and had numerous exhibits of her collection. In 1986 Mary was honored with Michigan Senate Resolution No. 605 honoring her for "many contri-butions to the art of quiltmaking."

The Kitty Clark Cole Collection

In 1991 Kitty Clark Cole took her first quiltmaking class, became immediately hooked, and started buying lots of fabric. By the mid-1990s, her interest had become so developed that, from December 1993 - December 1995, she owned and managed Village Patchwork. She also taught quilting classes for children and photo-transfer t-shirt quilt classes. Now, in addition to enjoying replicating antique quilts with repro-duction fabrics, Kitty lectures on quilt history and quilt care.

Kitty's first visit to the MSU Museum was to view an exhibit of the Clarke family quilt collection and to meet Kurt Dewhurst, the museum's director, and Marsha MacDowell, the curator of folk art. Kitty recalls, "Once I walked in the door, [saw the wonderful collection and] met Kurt and Marsha, well. . .the rest is history as they say. I guess we bonded." An active member of the Greater Ann Arbor Quilt Guild, she has served as guild president and chair of the Education and Preservation Committee. Currently she is a member of the board for The Alliance for American Quilts, a member of the MSU Museum's Development Council, and a leader in the formation of the Great Lakes Quilt Center.

Kitty purchased the first quilt for her collection in January, 1991. It was an appliquéd central medallion pieced by Shirley Shenk of Goshen, Indiana and quilted by Amish women from Goshen. She has since built a collection of outstanding quilts which reflect both her interests and the heritage of her family.

Kitty is especially fond of a bright golden-colored fabric known as "Cheddar" (because of its similarity to the color of Cheddar cheese and sometimes known as chrome orange or antimony). "Cheddar" was the most prominent color used in one of the quilts Kitty inherited from her great-grandmother Mary Jane "Bird" Jamison Clark and she has collected several quilts containing this fabric.

POSTAGE STAMP OR PHILADELPHIA PAVEMENT QUILT

Maker unknown; attributed to a Mennonite
c. 1890-1910
Bowmansville, Lancaster County, Pennyslvania
Cotton
73" x 76½"
Promised gift of Kitty Clark Cole
Photo by Mary Whalen

The striking graphic design of this quilt is typical of Pennsylvania quilts from this region and period. The pristine condition of this quilt provides a unique opportunity to enjoy the bright palette of its unusual setting and pieced border.

FOUR EAGLE QUILT

Maker unknown
c. 1860 -1890
Berks County, Pennsylvania
Cotton
84¹/₄" x 84¹/₄"
Promised gift of Kitty
Clark Cole
Photo by Mary Whalen

Among Kitty's special collecting interests are quilts with Cheddar fabric and those with patriotic motifs; this quilt contains both those elements. Kitty has collected several quilts in the four eagle pattern.

FRIENDSHIP OR SAMPLER QUILT

Made by friends and relatives of Annie Risser Horst
c. 1890
Middleton, Lancaster County, Pennsylvania
Cotton
78¹/₂" x 79"
Promised gift of Kitty
Clark Cole
Photo by Mary Whalen

Annie Risser Horst's Amish friends and family members made her this quilt. Names found on the quilt are Aunt Lorrie Risser, My mother G., Mother Risser, Mother Horst, Aunt Ella Horst, Edna Bachman Roy, and Sadie Risser. Amish rarely use printed fabric in their quilts; this quilt is an exception.

TOBACCO RIBBON QUILT

Maker unknown
c. 1890-1910
Provenance unknown
Silk ribbons on cotton
foundation squares
65¼" x 66¼"
Promised gift of
Kitty Clark Cole
Photo by Mary Whalen

During the late 19th and
early 20th century, novelty
fabrics were produced to help
promote the sale of tobacco.
The silk ribbons found in this
quilt would have been
wrapped around bundles of
cigars; the ribbons carry the
brand names of the cigars.

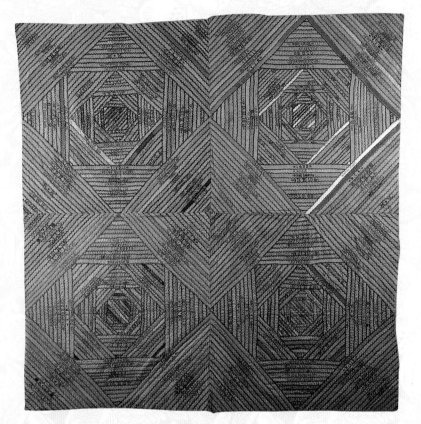

POSTAGE STAMP VARIABLE STAR QUILT

Mrs. Jacob Sauder (b. 1884,
death date unknown)
c. 1900
Churchtown, Lancaster
County, Pennsylvania
Cotton
86½" x 87"
Promised gift of
Kitty Clark Cole
Photo by Mary Whalen

Mrs. Sauder was described to
Kitty as an "Old Order
Mennonite" who made all of
her quilts entirely by hand.
This piece was reported to
have been made prior to her
marriage. Sauder passed it
on to her only daughter who
in turn gave it to her daughter.

LIBERTY TREE QUILT
(Pine Tree Quilt)

Mrs. S. K. Daniels
c. 1896
Purchased in Kentucky
Cotton
69" x 80½"
Promised gift of
Kitty Clark Cole
Photo by Mary Whalen

In her embroidered, signed, and dated work, Mrs. Daniels commemorates generals, politicians, and battles of the Civil War. In the center of the quilt she embroidered the words "Liberty Tree." Also found on the quilt is the phrase "abstain from strong drink" thus conveying the maker's convictions about temperance.

MARINER'S COMPASS QUILT

Maker unknown
c. 1850
Probably from Pennsylvania
Cotton
97½" x 100½"
Kitty Clark Cole Collection,
Promised gift of
Kitty Clark Cole
Photo by Mary Whalen

An outstanding example of trapunto and intricate hand piecing, the quilt includes stuffed designs of grapes, wreaths, tulips, roses, leaves, and other foliage. The quilt, which Kitty purchased in the Shenandoah Valley of Virginia, is in mint condition and pencil lines are still visible where the quilter marked the top.

MENNONITE PINEAPPLE QUILT
(Log Cabin Quilt)

Maker unknown
c. 1890
Saudertown, Bucks County,
Pennsylvania
Cotton
80³/₄" x 81"
Promised gift of
Kitty Clark Cole
Photo by Mary Whalen

This quilt offers a remarkable
fabric study of typical late
19th century fabrics. A
wide variety of shirtings,
double pinks, stripes, plaids,
"Hershey" browns, mourning
prints, and others create
an encyclopedia of the
era's textiles.

CHRISTMAS QUILT
(Floral Appliqué Quilt)

Maker unknown (signed
"____Neff")
1874
Possibly Pennsylvania
Cotton
78¹/₂" x 79"
Promised gift of
Kitty Clark Cole
Photo by Mary Whalen

Shortly after purchasing the
quilt, Kitty loaned this for an
exhibition the MSU Museum
mounted in conjunction with
the 1999 American Quilt
Study Group Seminar in East
Lansing, Michigan. Because
she had not yet had the
opportunity to examine the
quilt closely herself, she was
very pleased that, at the
exhibit, Xenia Cord and
Bettina Havig discovered the
"Neff" signature and the date
"1874" on the quilt.

MASONIC SYMBOL QUILT (Mosaic or Tile Quilt)

Maker unknown
c. 1920-1940
Provenance unknown
Cotton
67" x 83¼"
Promised gift of
Kitty Clark Cole
Photo by Mary Whalen

This free-style appliquéd quilt is rich in Masonic symbols including a square and compass with the letter "G," a scythe, Jacob's Ladder, and a pot of incense.

BIRDS IN THE AIR QUILT

Maker unknown
c. 1850-1880
Provenance unknown
Cotton, wool batting
90" x 90"
MSUM 6715.1; Gift of
Merry and Albert J. Silber
Photo by KEVA

This Birds in the Air quilt in the Barn Raising setting is made with madder-style prints. These prints, made to look like those earlier fabrics dyed with the root of the madder plant, were popular in the last half of the 19th century. The palette of madder-style prints resembled that of the paisley shawl, a very popular fashion accessory of the day.

HEXAGON MOSAIC QUILT

Maker unknown
c. 1840-1860
Provenance unknown
Cotton
70" x 80½"
MSUM 7024.1; Gift of
Merry and
Albert J. Silber
Photo by KEVA

The hexagon or honeycomb pattern found in this quilt was one of the first patterns to be named in a printed source. The maker used unusually tiny stitches, numbering 18 stitches to the inch, to assemble the blocks. The large-scale chintz used in the border has now lost its glaze, but it has been reproduced by RJR Fashion Fabrics.

BRODERIE PERSE QUILT

Maker unknown
c. 1840-1860
New York
Cotton
90" x 100"
MSUM 6981.2; Gift of
Merry and Albert J. Silber
Photo by Mary Whalen

This mint-condition, cut-out chintz appliqué quilt is an excellent example of how early 19th century quiltmakers could make expensive chintz fabrics go further to good effect. After 1858, textile manufacturers began producing less-expensive fabrics for the express purpose of using them on quilts in this manner.

CACTUS BASKET QUILT

Maker unknown
c. 1880-1900
Ohio or Pennsylvania
Cotton
74 1/2" x 78 1/2"
MSUM 6592.3; Gift of
Merry and Albert J. Silber
Photo by KEVA

No published copy of this
pattern, a variation on the
multitude of basket patterns,
is known and the pattern may
be unique. The quilt features
a variety of printed plaids,
checks, and small scale floral
prints. The binding and sashing are made from two different indigo blue prints.

FLYING GEESE QUILT

Maker unknown
c. 1840-1860
New England or
Pennsylvania
Cotton, wool, cotton batting
86" x 88"
MSUM 6521.1; Gift of Merry
and Albert J. Silber
Photo by KEVA

The unusual border fabric of
this quilt was made from
striped wool dress fabric
alternated between a printed
plaid stripe and a floral stripe
on a moiré backgound. This
fabric inspired a reproduction
produced by RJR Fashion
Fabrics featured in their
Great Lakes, Great Quilts line.

SAWTOOTH STAR QUILT

Maker unknown
c. 1830-1850
Provenance unknown
Cotton
87" x 103"
MSUM 6981.3; Gift of
Merry and Albert J. Silber
Photo by Mary Whalen

This quilt, containing 35 pieced muslin stars, each surrounded by a number of interesting prints, is a text-book for study of fabric from the 1840s-1850s. The sashing is a printed stripe of brown and vivid blue fabric, which contrasts nicely with the use of pink throughout the quilt. The wide chintz border still retains its glaze.

WHIG ROSE QUILT

Maker unknown
c. 1860
probably Pennsylvania
Cotton
89" x 90"
MSUM 1998:53.115; Mary
Schafer Quilt and Ephemera
Collection
Photo by KEVA

Mary Schafer collected a total of three quilts created in the Whig Rose or Democrat Rose pattern. The mustard-yellow print found in the background of this one is typical of a Pennsylvania Dutch quilt and the use of the large, four block appliqués set into four quadrants was common in the mid-19th century. The popularity of the Whig Rose quilting pattern persisted long after the Whig political party was challenged, and then disappeared during the mid-1800s.

WHOLE CLOTH QUILT

Theresa Hamilton
1837
Harpersfield [state unidentified]
Cotton with cotton stuffing
82" x 83"
MSUM 1998:53.116; Mary
Schafer Quilt and Ephemera
Collection
Photo by KEVA

As the supply of cotton
thread became greater and
less expensive after 1810, the
popularity of quilts featuring
stuffed (also called "trapunto") work increased.
Intricately stitched, these
textiles were a showcase for
the expert needlewoman.
This quilt is inscribed in
silk thread, "Theresa M.
Hamilton. October 8, 1837.
Harpersfield."

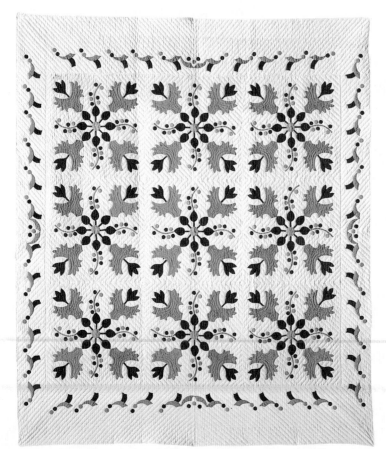

FLOWERING ALMOND QUILT

Betty Harriman (1890 -1971),
piecer; Mary Schafer
(b. 1910), quilter
1968-1971
Bunceton, Cooper County,
Missouri and Flushing,
Genessee County, Michigan
Cotton with polyester batting
83" x 96"
MSUM 1998.53.35; Mary
Schafer Quilt and Ephemera
Collection
Photo by KEVA

This appliqué design, a popular motif from the mid-19th
century, was one of Betty's
favorites. Part of the challenge posed to Mary as she
undertook the finishing of
Betty's work was trying to
complete the quilts in the
manner that Betty herself
would have. Mary has completed sixteen of Betty's
quilts; for Mary, this work
tightens the bond of friendship she shared with Betty.

STAR OF BETHLEHEM QUILT

Margaret (or Anna) David (Odawa)
ca. 1920
Peshawbestown, Leelanau County, Michigan
Cotton with cotton filling
76" x 91"
MSUM 6615.1; North American Indian and Native Hawaiian Quilt Collection,
Gift of Elizabeth and Vernon Keye
Photo © Peter Glendinning
For more information about this quilt, see p. 43

Star of Bethlehem

◀ Pattern by Beth Donaldson

Finished Size: 78" x 94"

FABRICS

2¾ yards green for A diamonds and appliqué

¾ yard second green for appliqué

⅛ yard striped shirting for B diamonds

1 yard purple for C diamonds

2 yards red for D diamonds and appliqué

1¼ yards pink for E diamonds

1¾ yards striped shirting for F diamonds

2¾ yards blue for G diamonds and outer border

1 yard bright pink for H diamonds and appliqué

1 yard yellow for I diamonds and appliqué

¾ yard deep red for J diamonds and appliqué

4 yards cream solid for appliqué backgrounds

¾ yard for binding

6 yards for backing

82" x 98" batting

STAR ASSEMBLY

1. Trim the width of each fabric to 30". Save the leftover pieces for the appliqué. Follow the chart to assign each fabric a letter and to cut the strips 1¾" wide:

Fabric color	Number of 1¾" strips
A Green	12
B Stripe shirting	2
C Purple	11
D Red	14
E Pink	17
F Striped shirting	26
G Blue	11
H Bright pink	8
I Yellow	15
J Deep red	5

2. Make 11 strip sets, each containing 11 strips. Sew the strips together as shown, following the chart order. Stagger each strip 1¾" as shown. Press the seam allowances of all odd numbered strip sets up and of all even numbered strip sets down.

Strip Sequence for Sets

Set 1: ABCDEFGHIFA

Set 2: BCDEFGHIFAE

Set 3: CDEFGHIFAED

Set 4: DEFGHIFAEDC

Set 5: EFGHIFAEDCF

Set 6: FGHIFAEDCFI

Set 7: GHIFAEDCFIJ

Set 8: HIFAEDCFIJG

Set 9: IFAEDCFIJGF

Set 10: FAEDCFIJGFE

Set 11: AEDCFIJGFED

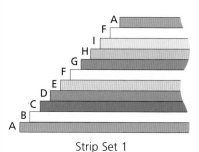

Strip Set 1

3. Trim the strip set at a 45° angle to even out the staggered edge. Use the 45° line on your ruler to keep the angle true. Make your next cut 1¾" from the trimmed edge. Continue cutting every 1¾" for a total of 8 segments (one for each star point). You will need to periodically re-align the 45° line to ensure perfect diamonds.

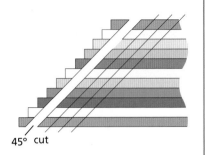

45° cut

Tips on Making Strip Sets:

Cut straight strips. Use a consistent $1/4$" seam allowance. Finger press before iron pressing all seams in the same direction. Press in a straight line to avoid bowing.

4. Use one segment from each of the 11 strips sets to make a star point. Align and mark the intersection of the seams $1/4$" from the cut edge. Pin, sew, and press.

Follow the illustration for the order to sew your sets. As you press, keep in mind this should be a true 45° diamond when finished. Be gentle while handling the bias edges (especially during pressing) to ensure the quilt lies flat when finished.

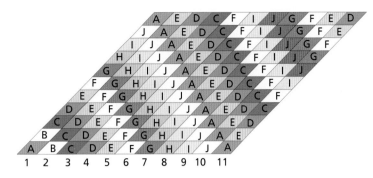

Star Point
Make 8

5. Sew the points together into pairs to make 4 quarters. Sew from seam line to seam line, stopping and starting $1/4$" from each end and backstitching at the beginning and end of each seam. This is a good time to check your work. The angle at the center of the star should be 90° and the points should lie flat. Press all the seams in the same direction (clockwise or counter clockwise).

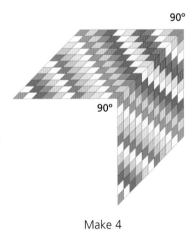

Make 4

6. Sew the quarters together to form the 2 halves, and then sew the final center seam. The star should lie flat.

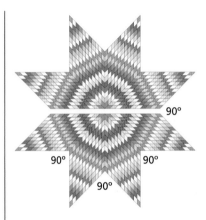

Appliqué Assembly

Refer to the Appliqué Appendix, page 91.

Use your favorite method of appliqué with the patterns provided on pages 92 and 93. Part of the appeal of the Native-American quilts is their folk-art quality, so feel free to alter the provided patterns a little and give yourself permission to trust your instincts.

1. Use the cutting diagrams on page 42 as a guide to cut your background fabrics. Lightly draw the shapes on the wrong side of your background fabric. Add 1" all around each shape and cut. This will allow for slight adjustments as needed.

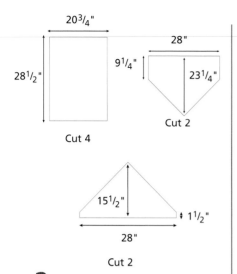

20³/₄"

28¹/₂"

Cut 4

28"

9¹/₄"

23¹/₄"

Cut 2

15¹/₂"

1¹/₂"

28"

Cut 2

2. Follow the appliqué placement diagram to arrange your appliqués. To capture the spontaneity of the original quilt, place the B and C circles by eye and play with the rotation of the A and D flowers.

3. After the appliqués are complete, press the backgrounds, then cut away any fabric behind the appliqués. Re-draw the background shapes to the sizes given. Add ¹/₄" around your newly drawn lines and cut.

QUILT ASSEMBLY

1. Refer to the quilt illustrations and sew the backgrounds to the star. Sew only from seam line to seam line, backstitching at the beginning and end of each seam. Be careful not to stretch the bias edges. Sew the extended setting triangles first. Notice the tips of the star "float" in the background fabric.

2. Sew the 4 rectangles last. The edges of the rectangles align exactly with the edges of the extended setting triangles to make the edges of the quilt top.

3. Cut eight border strips 4¹/₂" wide. Piece end-to-end to make two 4¹/₂" x 78" borders and two 4¹/₂" x 85¹/₂" borders. Sew border to quilt sides and then top and bottom. Press toward borders.

QUILTING

1. Layer top with backing and batting, and quilt. The original quilt has an overall Baptist Fan pattern (see page 54).

2. To finish, trim to square up the quilt and attach binding.

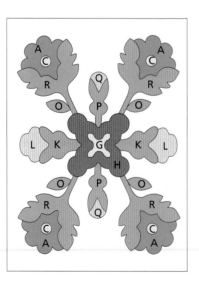

Make 4

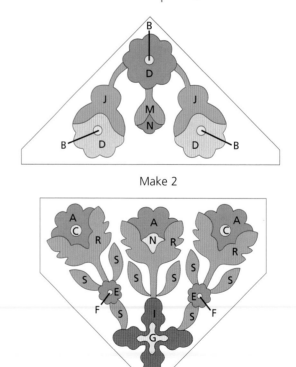

Make 2

Make 2

STAR OF BETHLEHEM QUILT PROJECT

Beth Donaldson, designer, machine piecer and machine appliquér;
Kari Ruedisale, machine quilter
2001
Lansing, Ingham County, Michigan
Cotton with cotton/polyester filling
78" x 94"
MSUM Teaching Collection
Photo by Mary Whalen

The reproduction of this traditional Lone Star is made easier by using rotary cutting and strip piecing techniques as well as machine piecing, appliquéing, and quilting. The fabrics of the original were calicos typical of the era and it is easy today to find similar reproductions. The appliqué shapes are all slightly different in the original. Irregularity in the shapes and placements of the Woodland flowers are part of this quilt's original appeal and it is best not to be too exact when cutting, laying out, and sewing them in the reproduction.

The original quilt is similar to several others made in the early 20th century by Native American women from Leelanau County, Michigan. It is probable that Native Americans began quilting in the Great Lakes region after the establishment of Catholic missions in the 19th century; it is known that quilting took place at the Immaculate Conception in Peshawbestown. According to James M. McClurken, co-author with James A. Clifton and George L. Cornell, of *People of the Three Fires: The Ottawa, Potawatomi, and Ojibway of Michigan,* the star and floral motifs used in this quilt are typical components of Ottawa (Odawa) designs and mimic designs depicted in earlier porcupine quill work and beaded pieces of the region.

UNDERGROUND RAILROAD OR GRANDMOTHER'S FAN VARIATION

Myla Perkins (b. 1939)
1984
Detroit, Wayne County, Michigan
Cotton/polyester with polyester filling
69" x 90"
MSUM 7421.1; Michigan African-American Quilt Collection
Photo by Mark Eifert
For more information about this quilt, see p. 47

Underground Railroad

◀ Pattern by Beth Donaldson

Finished Quilt Size: $72^1/_2$" x $96^1/_2$"

Finished Block Size: 12"

FABRICS

$4^1/_4$ yards cream solid for corners and background of Fan blocks, and background of Underground Railroad blocks

3 yards light turquoise for alternating blocks and fan blades

$2^1/_4$ yards medium turquoise for the Underground Railroad block and fan blades

1 yard navy for the fan blades

$^3/_4$ yards binding

$5^3/_4$ yards backing

77" x 101" batting

Template plastic

GRANDMOTHER'S FAN BLOCK ASSSEMBLY

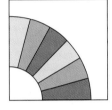

Make 28

1. Enlarge and trace the patterns A, B, C (pages 94) on to template plastic and carefully cut them out.

2. For each fan cut 2 light turquoise, 2 medium turquoise, and 2 navy blades; cut one fan corner and one fan background from cream. You will need 56 total of each color of fan blade and 28 corners and backgrounds for the entire quilt.

3. Sew the fan blades together side by side. Press seams in one direction.

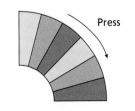

Press

4. Sew the fan corner to the blade bottoms and sew the fan background to the fan tops. Press seams toward background. Make 28 fan blocks that measure $12^1/_2$" square, including seam allowances.

UNDERGROUND RAILROAD BLOCK ASSEMBLY

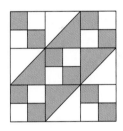

Make 8

1. To make Four-Patch blocks, cut five $2^1/_2$"-wide strips each of medium turquoise and cream fabric. Sew pairs of strips together and press toward the medium fabric. Cut each strip into $2^1/_2$" segments to make 80 units. Sew the units together in pairs, as shown. Press. Make 40 Four-Patches that measure $4^1/_2$" including seam allowances.

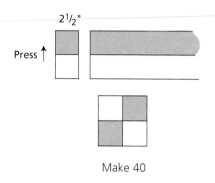

2½"

Press ↑

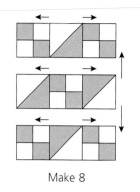

Make 40

2. To make half-square triangles, cut sixteen 4⅞" squares of medium and sixteen 4⅞" squares of cream fabric. On the wrong side of the lighter fabrics, draw one diagonal line. With right sides together layer one cream square and one medium square, then sew ¼" from both sides of the diagonal line. Cut apart on the drawn line. Press toward the medium fabric. Make thirty-two half-square triangle squares that measure 4½" including seam allowances.

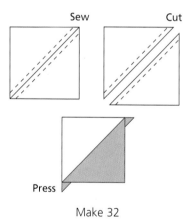

Sew   Cut

Press

Make 32

3. Lay out all the units for one block, as shown. Sew and press according to the diagram. Make a total of eight Underground Railroad blocks that measure 12½" including seam allowances.

Make 8

Quilt Assembly

1. Cut twelve 12½" squares of light turquoise fabric.

2. Referring to the quilt photograph, lay out your blocks. Sew the blocks together into horizontal rows. Press seams of each row in alternate direction.

3. Sew the rows together to complete the top. Press.

Quilting

1. Layer top with backing and batting and quilt. The original quilt has outline quilting in the Underground Railroad blocks and the fan blades. In the 4 corners where the fans stop, a fan outline is quilted in the light block. Circular echo quilting 1" apart is used throughout the rest of the quilt.

2. To finish, trim to square up the quilt and attach binding.

To produce the navy and yellow version: Substitute navy fabrics for all the backgrounds and corners of the fans and all the alternate blocks. Make all the fan blades yellow. Make all the half-square triangles yellow and white. Make 24 of the four patches navy and light blue and 16 of the four patches navy and yellow.

UNDERGROUND RAILROAD QUILT PROJECT

Beth Donaldson, designer and piecer; John Putnam, machine quilter
2001
Lansing, Ingham County, Michigan
Cotton with cotton/polyester filling
$72^1/_2$" x $96^1/_2$"
MSUM Teaching Collection
Photo by Mary Whalen

The design is a dynamic combination of plain blocks and pieced blocks in the Underground Railroad (also called Jacob's Ladder) and Grandmother's Fan patterns. The colors of the original quilt are soft and lovely and, since the original was made relatively recently, it is fairly easy to find fabrics to duplicate it. Beth thought it would be interesting to reverse the color palette in the reproduction to show a different view of the quilt. To add variety and show a scrappy approach as well, she placed her blocks of soft blues and a full range of yellows on a background of several different deep navies.

The original quilt was made by Myla Perkins and her sister Clara Clark, along with Elva Gamble, Gwen Spears, and another set of sisters, Charlesetta Buie and Elizabeth Jaggers, the original members of the Detroit group, The Quilting Six Plus. Jaggers said that when the group first got together in the late 1980s, family and friends doubted that "six beautiful, intelligent black women were getting together to quilt." When The Quilting Six Plus held their own exhibit and displayed more than 70 quilts, visitors were impressed and many asked to join the group. Myla Perkins named her variation of the Jacob Ladder pattern the Underground Railroad quilt. Its name had nothing to do with the widely-circulated but currently unsubstantiated story that certain quilt patterns were used as signs for travelers on the Underground Railroad.

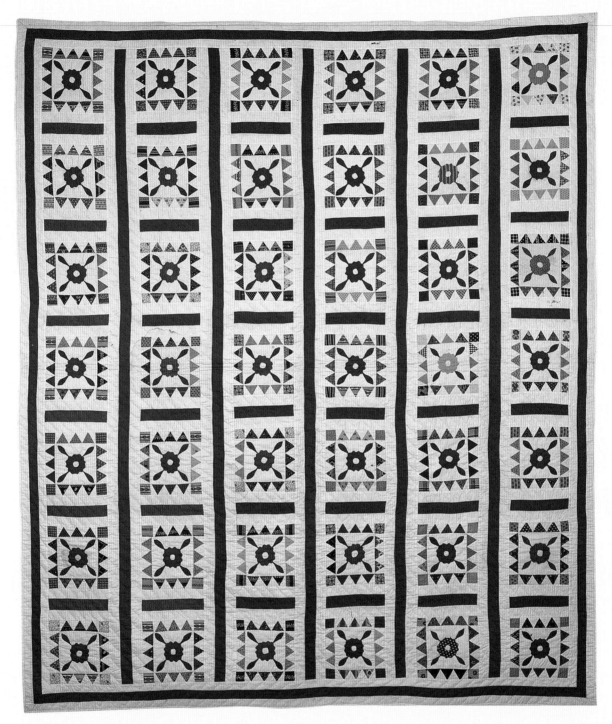

ROSE IN THE WINDOW QUILT

Maker unknown
ca. 1860
Found in Michigan
Cotton with cotton filling
69" x 82"
MSUM 7610.1; Gift of Merry and Albert J. Silber
Photo by Mary Whalen
For more information about this quilt, see p. 51

Rose In the Window

◀ Pattern by Beth Donaldson

Finished Quilt Size: 84$\frac{1}{2}$" x 104$\frac{3}{4}$"

Finished Block Size: 7$\frac{1}{8}$"

FABRICS

Use reproduction fabrics from pre-Civil War fabric lines as your guide.

9$\frac{1}{4}$ yards cream solid for backgrounds, sawtooth borders and sashings

2 yards red solid for sashings

1 yard total assorted scrap prints and solids for flowers. The original quilt features mostly solid reds, while the reproduction quilt has mostly prints. Each quilt also has an occasional golden yellow or pink flower.

$\frac{1}{2}$ yard total assorted prints for green leaves

3$\frac{3}{4}$ yards total assorted prints for Sawtooth borders

$\frac{3}{4}$ yard for binding

7$\frac{1}{2}$ yards for backing

89" x 109" batting

Template plastic

The yardage and instructions given are for the reproduction quilt found on page 51.

CUTTING

Cream solid:

Cut twelve 5$\frac{1}{2}$"-wide strips, then cut the strips into eighty 5$\frac{1}{2}$" squares.

Cut eighty-six 1$\frac{1}{2}$"-wide strips.

Red solid:

Cut forty-three 1$\frac{1}{2}$"-wide strips.

BLOCK ASSEMBLY

Refer to the Appliqué Appendix, page 91.

1. In preparation for appliqué, finger press each 5$\frac{1}{2}$" cream square, as shown. Use the finger-creased lines to help center the flower and place the leaves.

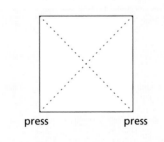

press   press

2. Use your favorite method of appliqué with the rose and leaf patterns on page 93. Make 80 roses and 320 leaves.

3. Place 4 leaves and 1 flower on the square. Align leaf tips with finger creases as shown. Appliqué in place.

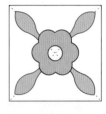

Make 80

4. Trim the block to 5" square keeping the appliqué centered on the cream square.

5. To make Sawtooth border, trace patterns A, B, and C onto template plastic (page 93). Reverse C to make Cr.

For each block cut 4 A's and 12 B's of printed fabric. Cut 8 B's, 4 C's, and 4 Cr's from the cream background fabric.

6. Sew B's, C's, and Cr's together as shown to make 4 Sawtooth strips for each block. Press.

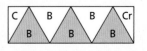

7. Sew the 4 A's to opposite ends of 2 strips. Press toward A's.

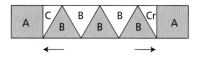

8. Match up edges and seams and sew the Sawtooth strips to the appliqué square, as shown. Press seams toward the appliqué square. The block now measures $7^5/_8$" square including seam allowances.

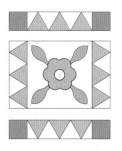

SASHING AND BORDER ASSEMBLY

1. Sew three $1^1/_2$"-wide cream strips end-to-end to make a long strip (about 120"). Repeat for a total of 18 long cream strips.

2. Sew three $1^1/_2$"-wide red strips end-to-end to make a long strip (about 120"). Repeat for a total of 9 long red strips.

3. Sew one long cream strip on both sides of a red strip. Press toward the red strip, keeping the strips as straight as possible. Trim the length of each set to about 108" to make a total of 9 vertical sashing units.

4. Cut the leftover strip sets from Step 3 into $7^5/_8$" horizontal sashing units.

5. To make the remaining horizontal sashing units, you will need thirty-two $1^1/_2$"-wide strips from the cream fabric, and sixteen $1^1/_2$"-wide strips from the red fabric.

6. Sew one cream strip on both sides of a red strip. Press toward the red strip, keeping the strips as straight as possible. Make a total of 16 strip sets.

7. Cut the strip sets into $7^5/_8$" horizontal sashing units. Add these to the units from Step 4 for a total of 88.

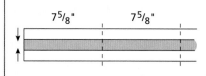

QUILT ASSEMBLY

1. Sew one horizontal sashing unit to the top of each appliqué sawtooth block. Press toward the sashing.

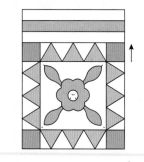

2. Arrange the blocks in a pleasing manner, 8 blocks across and 10 blocks down.

3. Sew the blocks into vertical rows and add a horizontal sashing strip to the bottom of each row. Refer to the quilt photograph on page 51.

4. Measure each row. They should be the same, $104^3/_4$". If they are close, use the average length. If there is more than $1/_2$" difference, make minor adjustments in the seams of a few horizontal sashing strips until all the rows measure within $1/_4$" of each other.

5. Trim the vertical sashing strips to the length you calculated in Step 4 (it should be $104^3/_4$").

6. Sew the vertical sashing strips to the rows according to the photograph on page 51 and press toward the sashing.

QUILTING AND FINISHING

1. Layer top with batting and backing. Quilt in the ditch around the appliqués and Sawtooths. Quilt in 1" diagonal lines in the vertical and horizontal sashings.

2. To finish, trim to square up the quilt and attach binding.

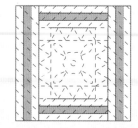

Quilting for *Rose in the Window*

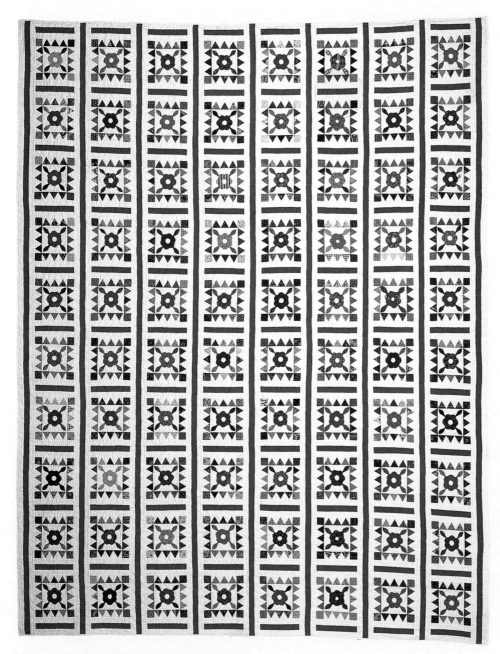

ROSE IN THE WINDOW QUILT PROJECT

The MSU Museum Quilters
2000
Lansing, Ingham County, Michigan
Cotton with cotton filling
84" x 104"
Owned by April Yorks,
Flint, Michigan
Photo by Mary Whalen

This quilt was made by the MSU Museum Quilters for a raffle to raise funds to benefit the MSU Museum's quilt collection. The MSU Museum quilters were a loosely-organized group that, between 1999 and 2000, made 13 quilts for Safe House (the first domestic abuse shelter on a college campus) and this raffle quilt. Members of this group, led by Beth Donaldson, included, Norine Antuck, Marge Dickinson, Nancy Bekofske, Geri Smith, Barb Worthington, Kate Edgar, Mary Edgar, Fran Tyndale, Ruby Post, Pat Clark, Carol Schon, Lennie Rathbun, Jackie Shulsky, Jane Roehm, Marie VanTilburg, Peggy Bollaert, and Bonnie Bus. Donaldson drafted and gave the quilters the pattern for the quilt block and told them to use any fabric they thought looked old. It is always interesting to see how such a brief instruction on color can produce such terrific results. To make the quilt more appealing to ticket buyers, the quilt was made queen size by increasing the original number of blocks from 42 to 80. The scale of the blocks and sashings were unchanged.

The Museum staff determined that the original quilt was ca. 1860 date by an examination of the prints used in the sawtooths on each block. The combination of a simple appliqué surrounded by 60-degree triangles is unusual and the only one like it in the MSUM collection; it may be a completely unique pattern. Donor Merry Silber named the pattern Rose in the Window because the flowers are a typical Rose of Sharon pattern and the sawtooths framed each flower.

String Plate Quilt

Ethel West Adair (1901-1993)
1940s-1950s
Oklahoma
Cotton
67" x 84$\frac{1}{2}$"
MSUM 2000:1.1; North American Indian and Native Hawaiian Quilt
Collection, Gift of Lynda Chenoweth
Photo by Mary Whalen
For more information about this quilt, see p. 55

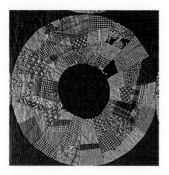

String Plate

◀ Pattern by Mary Worrall

Finished Quilt Size: 80" x 100"

Finished Block Size: 20"

FABRICS

11 yards total assorted scrap fabrics for plates. If you are not working from scraps, $1/8$ yard cuts work well.

$7 3/4$ yards for foundation (muslin recommended)

$5 3/4$ yards red for background

$3/4$ yard for binding

6 yards for backing

84" x 104" batting

Template plastic

CUTTING

Plate Fabric:

Cut scraps into pieces $5 1/2$" long and ranging from $3/4$" to $2 1/2$" wide.

Foundation:

Cut fifty-two $4 1/2$"-wide strips.

Background:

Cut ten $20 1/2$"-wide strips, then cut the strips into twenty $20 1/2$" squares.

STRING PIECING

The plate sections are pieced using improvisational string piecing which is a stitch and flip method using a foundation.

1. Start piecing at one end of a foundation strip. Place your first piece of plate fabric right side up on the foundation fabric.

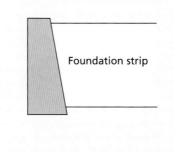

Foundation strip

2. Place your second piece of plate fabric on piece 1 right side sides together. Sew a $1/4$" seam. Flip piece 2 to its right side and finger press.

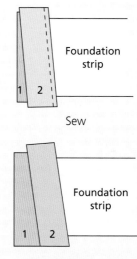

Foundation strip

Sew

Foundation strip

Flip and finger press

3. Continue adding plate fabric strips in this manner until the strip of foundation fabric is covered. Vary the widths of the plate fabric strips. You can also vary the angles at which you add plate fabric strips to the foundation. Piece all foundation strips.

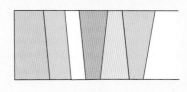

4. Enlarge and trace the wedge pattern on page 95 onto template plastic.

5. Use the template to cut the plate wedges as shown. Eighteen wedges are needed per plate; 360 wedges total.

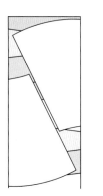

BLOCK ASSEMBLY

1. Sew the wedges together as shown. Press the seams open. Continue sewing until you have sewn 9 wedges together. This is half of the plate unit. Repeat to make the other half.

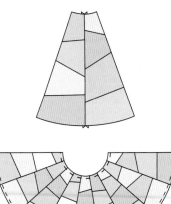

One half of the plate; make 40

2. Sew the 2 halves of the plate together. Press the seams open. Make 20 plates.

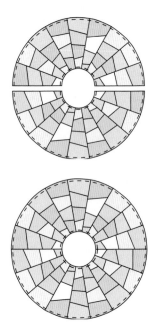

Make 20

3. Center the plate onto a square of background fabric. Appliqué as desired to the background squares. The reproduction quilt was machine appliquéd using a buttonhole stitch. Make 20 blocks.

QUILT ASSEMBLY

Sew blocks into rows, pressing all seams in the first row in one direction. In the second row, press all seams in the opposite direction. The quilt is 4 blocks across by 5 blocks down.

QUILTING AND FINISHING

1. Layer top, batting, and backing; quilt. The quilting on the original quilt is in a fan design.

2. To finish, trim to square up the quilt and attach binding.

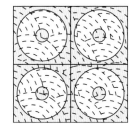

Fan quilting design

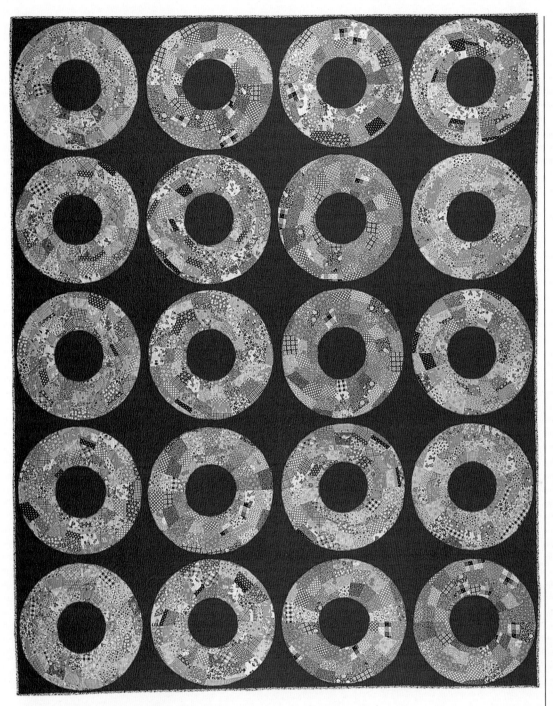

The project for the String Plate Quilt was made in a palette similar to Ethel Adair's original piece. The plates were pieced from the many reproductions of fabrics from the 1930s and 1940s which are available on today's market. Brights or batiks against a black background fabric would be an interesting alternative for piecing the quilt.

Circular patterns like this one are known not only as Dresden Plate but also as Wagon Wheel or Wheel of Fortune. The string piecing in the wheel spokes of this particular quilt, however, is unusual. Similar to crazy quilting, string piecing traditionally involves sewing pieces of fabric onto a fabric or paper foundation. The technique allows a quilter to make use of small or oddly shaped pieces of fabric which are not suitable for more regular patchwork. It more commonly appears in quilts as simple square blocks or as large eight-pointed stars.

STRING PLATE QUILT PROJECT

Mary Worrall, designer and piecer; Kari Ruedisale, quilter
Made 2001
East Lansing, Ingham County, Michigan
Cotton with cotton/polyester batting
72" x 90"
MSUM Teaching Collection
Photo by Mary Whalen

BAR SAMPLER QUILT

Maker unknown
Made ca. 1890
Provenance unknown
Cotton with cotton filling
77" x 84"
MSUM 3694.1; Gift of Dr. Paul Love
Photo by KEVA
For more information about this quilt, see p. 61

Bar Sampler

◀ Pattern by Beth Donaldson

Finished Block Sizes: large Nine-Patch $6^3/8$"

small Nine-Patch $4^1/2$"

Eliza's Star $4^1/2$"

Jack Knife variation $6^3/8$"

Double X $6^3/8$"

FABRICS

1 yard red print fabric for the setting triangles in the center strip

$1^3/4$ yards second red print for the setting triangles in the outer strips

$2/3$ yard blue for the inner strips

$2/3$ yard pink for the inner strips

$3/4$ yard tan for the outer strips

See individual block assembly for the block yardages.

Have fun with your scraps and throw in some unexpected colors, too!

$3/4$ yard for binding

$4^3/4$ yards for backing

81" x 86" batting

DOUBLE X BLOCK ASSEMBLY

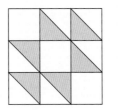

Double X Block
Make 19

Brown scraps to total $1/2$ yard

Tan scraps to total 1 yard

For one block:

1. Cut three $2^5/8$" squares of tan fabric.

2. Cut three 3" squares each of tan fabric and brown fabric.

3. To make half-square triangles, draw a diagonal line on the wrong side of each tan square. With right sides together layer one tan with one brown and sew $1/4$" from both sides of the diagonal line. Cut apart on the drawn line. Press toward the brown triangle to make six $2^5/8$" half-square triangles including seam allowances. Trim any tips. Make six for each block, 114 total.

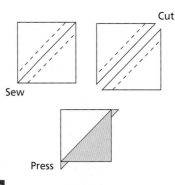

Cut

Sew

Press

4. Lay out the half-square triangles with the tan squares. Sew and press, as shown. The block measures $6^7/8$" square including seam allowances. Make 19 total Double X blocks.

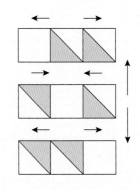

5. Cut two of the Double X blocks in half on the diagonal, as shown on page 58. Mark the diagonal line, measure $1/4$" beyond that line, and cut. This allows for a seam allowance when assembling the quilt.

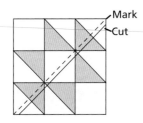

Cut two blocks in half

JACK KNIFE VARIATION BLOCK ASSEMBLY

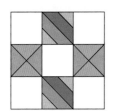

Jack Knife Variation Block
Make 16

Shirting scraps to total $1/2$ yard

Red scraps to total $3/4$ yard

Green scraps to total $3/8$ yard

Blue scraps to total $1/4$ yard

Brown scraps to total $3/8$ yard

Add bits of yellow and deep red, too!

For one block:

1. Cut five $2^5/8$" squares of shirting.

2. Cut one $3^3/8$" square each of red and green. To make the quarter-square triangles, draw two diagonal lines on the wrong side of the lighter fabric. With right sides together, layer the squares and sew $1/4$" from both sides of one of the diagonal lines. Cut apart on both diagonal

lines to make 4 triangle units. Press toward the red fabrics. Pair the triangle units and sew to make two $2^5/8$" squares.

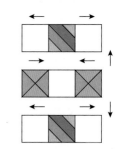

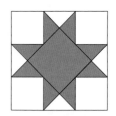

Make 2 for each block; 32 total

3. Cut two $1^3/8$" x 8" strips of red. Cut one $1^1/4$" x 8" strip each of blue and brown. Sew the strips together with the $1^3/8$"-wide strips on the outside edges. Press the seams in one direction. Align the center seam with the diagonal lines of a rotary cutting square as shown and cut two $2^5/8$" squares.

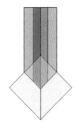

Make 2 for each block; 32 total

4. Lay out all the units. Sew and press, as shown. The block measures $6^7/8$" square including seam allowances. Make 16 total Jack Knife variation blocks.

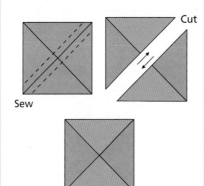

AUNT ELIZA'S STAR BLOCK ASSEMBLY

Aunt Eliza's Star
Make 6 total (4 red and 2 navy)

Shirting scraps to total $1/4$ yard

Navy scraps to total $1/4$ yard

Red scraps to total $1/4$ yard

For each block:

1. Cut four 2" squares of shirting fabric. Cut one $2^5/8$" square of navy or red.

2. Cut one $2^3/4$" square each of shirting fabric and navy or red fabric. On the wrong side of the shirting fabric, draw 2 diagonal lines. With right sides together layer the squares and sew $1/4$" from both sides of one of the diagonal lines. Cut apart on both drawn diagonal lines to make four units. Press toward the dark fabric.

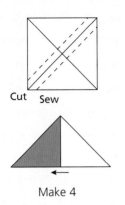

Cut   Sew

Make 4

3. Sew the above units to adjacent sides of 2 of the shirting squares, as shown. Press away from the shirting square.

Make 2

4. Cut one $2^3/_4$" square of navy or red fabric. Cut on the diagonal twice to make 4 triangles. Sew two triangles to adjacent sides of the last 2 squares of shirting. Press away from the shirting fabric.

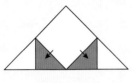

Make 2

5. Lay out all the units. Sew and press as shown. The block measures 5" square including seam allowances. Make 4 navy and two red Eliza Star blocks.

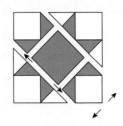

SMALL NINE-PATCH BLOCKS

Nine-Patch Block
Make 20

Fabric requirements:

Shirting fabrics to total $1/_3$ yard

Blue, navy, red and green fabric scraps to total $1/_3$ yard

For one block:

1. Cut four 2" squares of dark fabric and five 2" squares of shirting fabric.

2. Lay out all the units. Sew and press as shown. The block measures 5" square including seam allowances. Make 20 total.

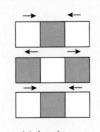

Make three

LARGE NINE-PATCH BLOCKS

Nine-Patch Block
Make 3

Use scraps from yardages left over from the other quilt blocks.

1. Cut twelve $2^5/_8$" squares of red and fifteen $2^5/_8$" squares of shirting fabric.

2. Lay out all the units. Sew and press as shown for small Nine-Patch blocks to make 3 Nine-Patch blocks measuring $6^7/_8$" including seam allowances.

3. Cut 2 of the blocks in half on the diagonal line, as shown. Mark the diagonal line, measure $1/_4$" beyond that line, and cut. This allows for a seam allowance when assembling the quilt.

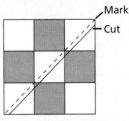

Cut two blocks in half

Quilt Assembly

1. For the setting triangles in the center strips with the Jack-Knife Variation and the large Nine-Patch blocks, cut nine $10^1/_4$" squares of red print. Cut each square on the diagonal twice to yield 36 large triangles (only 34 will be used). Cut two $5^3/_8$" squares of red print. Cut each on the diagonal once to yield 4 small triangles.

Cut on diagonal twice

Cut on diagonal once

2. For the strips with the Double X blocks, cut the nine $10^1/_4$" squares of a second red print. Cut each square on the diagonal twice to yield 36 large triangles (only 34 will be used). Cut two $5^3/_8$" squares of the second red print. Cut each in half diagonally to yield 4 small triangles.

3. For the outer strips with the smaller blocks, cut twelve $7^5/_8$" squares of the second red print. Cut each on the diagonal twice to yield 48 large triangles.

Cut four $4^1/_8$" squares of the second red print, and cut on the diagonal to make 8 small triangles.

4. Refer to the diagrams and to the quilt photograph to arrange the blocks and sew the strips. Press toward the setting triangles. Blocks and triangles are sewn to form diagonal units that are then sewn to make the whole strip. For the strips using the large blocks, add the half blocks as shown to create strips. Make the strips using the small blocks longer and trim to equal large block strips.

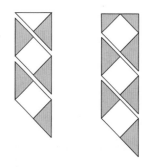

Adding setting squares
to make strips

5. Cut four $4^1/_2$"-wide strips of each of the light blue and pink fabric. Piece end-to-end to make 2 blue and 2 pink strips at least 82" long. Cut 4 tan strips $5^1/_2$" wide. Piece end-to-end to make 2 tan strips at least 82" long. Alternate the block strips with the plain strips referring to the quilt photograph on page 61. Keep the top edge even and press toward the plain strips. Trim the bottom edge even with the shortest strip. The quilt should measure about $75^1/_2$" x $81^1/_2$".

Quilting and Finishing

1. Layer top with batting and backing and quilt. Follow the diagram for the overall grid quilting and for placement of the leaves in the setting triangles.

2. To finish, trim to square up the quilt and attach binding.

Quilting design

BAR SAMPLER QUILT PROJECT

Beth Donaldson, designer; The Wednesday Group, machine piecer;
Kari Ruedisale, machine quilter
2001
Lansing, Ingham County, Michigan
Cotton with cotton/polyester filling
76" x 81"
MSUM Teaching Collection
Photo by Mary Whalen

When quilt samples are made for a book, the author/artist often relies heavily on friends to help out. Beth Donaldson took one look at the Bar Sampler and knew it was a perfect project for her pals, the Wednesday Group. The core remains strong with a shared fondness for "old-looking quilts." Those who made this top are Pat Clark, Pat Linnell, Jackie Shulsky, Marie VanTilburg, Carol Schon, Beth Donaldson, and Norine Antuck.

For this project, Beth tried to be as faithful as possible to the original colors used. In some cases, exposed seams made it easy for her to determine how much a color had faded, in other areas she had to guess. Beth enjoyed this project: "We found it fun to compare the reproduction with its crisp shirtings, double pink and soft blue strips, and strong red setting triangles to the well-used original. The quilt block in the center is also one that we couldn't find documented in our sources. The closest we could come was a Jack Knife variation."

Little is known about the provenance of the original quilt but, based on an examination of its fabrics, the museum staff estimates it to be c. 1890.

Even though the quilt is faded and has damage, it is an interesting example of the pattern because of the way in which the maker set the blocks on point, changed the scale of the blocks from the interior to the exterior strips, and used a zigzag setting in the center.

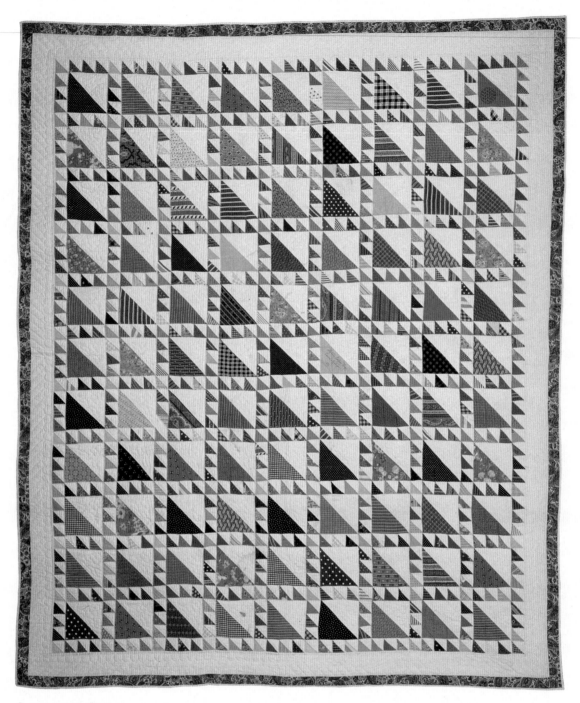

Sawtooth Quilt

Matilda Vary, piecer; Mary Schafer (b. 1910), finisher; Ida Pullum,
quilter
Top ca. 1876, finished ca. 1980
Top: Ceresco, Calhoun County, Michigan; finishing: Flushing,
Michigan
Cotton with polyester batting
$81^1/_4$" x 97"
MSUM 1998:53.86; Quilt from the Mary Schafer Collection
Photo by Mary Whalen

For more information about this quilt, see p. 65

Sawtooth

◀ Pattern by Mary Worrall

Finished Quilt Size: 86" x 102"

Finished Block Size: 8"

FABRICS

$4^1/_2$ yards light prints for Sawtooth backgrounds

$4^1/_2$ yards total assorted dark prints for Sawtooths

$1^3/_8$ yards light fabric for first border

$3/_4$ yard dark print for second border

$3/_4$ yard for binding

$7^1/_2$ yards for backing

90" x 106" batting

Collect a large variety of prints to achieve a scrap look in the quilt. The original quilt features up to 8 different prints within a single block. If you are purchasing fabric, you can use ten $^1/_4$ yard cuts for piece B and thirty-one $^1/_8$ yard cuts for piece D.

CUTTING

From Light:

Piece A:

Cut ten $6^7/_8$"-wide strips. Cut the strips into fifty $6^7/_8$" squares.

Piece C:

Cut thirty $2^7/_8$"-wide strips. Cut the strips into three hundred eighty-seven $2^7/_8$" squares.

From Dark:

Piece B:

Cut ten $6^7/_8$"-wide strips. Cut the strips into fifty $6^7/_8$" squares.

Piece D:

Cut thirty $2^7/_8$"-wide strips. Cut the strips into three hundred eighty-seven $2^7/_8$" squares.

First border:

Cut nine $4^1/_2$"-wide strips. Piece end-to-end and cut two $90^1/_2$"-long strips for the side borders and two $82^1/_2$"-long strips for the top and bottom borders.

Second border:

Cut ten $2^1/_2$"-wide strips. Piece end-to-end and cut two $98^1/_2$"-long strips for the side borders and two $86^1/_2$"-long strips for the top and bottom borders.

BLOCK ASSEMBLY

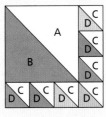

Sawtooth Block
Make 99

1. To make half-square triangle A/B unit, layer one dark $6^7/_8$" square and one $6^7/_8$" light square right sides together. Draw a line diagonally from corner to corner. Sew $1/_4$" from both sides of the line. Cut square in half along the drawn line. Press toward the darker fabric. Make one A/B unit for each block, 99 total.

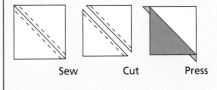

Sew   Cut   Press

2. To make half-square triangle C/D unit, layer one dark $2^7/_8$" square and one light $2^7/_8$" square right sides together. Mark, sew, and cut, as for A/B unit. Make seven C/D units for each block, 693 total. Make an additional 81 units for the border.

3. Sew three C/D units together, as shown. To create a scrappier look, use C/D units that are made of different fabrics. Press toward darker fabric. Make a total of 99.

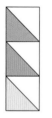

4. Sew 4 C/D units together, as shown. Press toward darker fabric. Make a total of 99.

5. Sew the three-C/D unit strip to the right side of A/B unit, as shown. Press toward A/B unit.

6. Sew the four-C/D unit strip to the bottom of unit A/B, as shown. Press toward unit A/B.

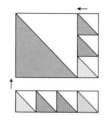

QUILT ASSEMBLY

1. Lay out the blocks, putting 9 blocks across by 11 blocks down. When you have a pleasing arrangement, sew the blocks together into horizontal rows. Press seams of each row in alternate directions. Sew the rows together.

2. To create the left column of half-square triangle units, sew together 44 C/D units. Attach to left side of quilt.

3. To create the top row of half-square triangles, sew together 37 of C/D units. Attach to top of quilt.

4. To make the first border, sew the $4^1/_2$" x $90^1/_2$" strips to the sides and the $4^1/_2$" x $82^1/_2$" strips to the top and bottom of the quilt top.

5. To make the second border, sew the $2^1/_2$" x $98^1/_2$" strips to the sides and the $2^1/_2$" x $86^1/_2$" strips to the top and bottom of the quilt top.

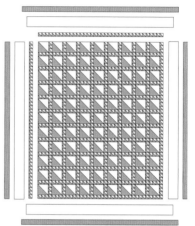

QUILTING AND FINISHING

1. Layer top, backing, and batting, the quilt. Quilting suggestions from the original quilt are shown in the illustration below. Pattern for flower is on page 94.

2. To finish, trim to square up the quilt and attach binding.

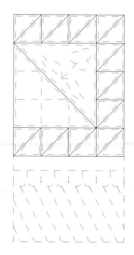

Quilting design

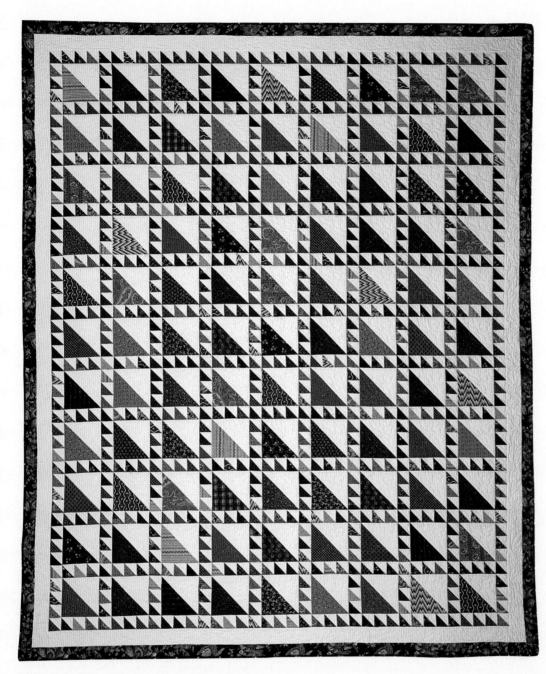

The Sawtooth quilt is a great opportunity to use up scrap fabric. The greater number of $2^{7}/_{8}$" and $6^{7}/_{8}$" squares you have, the "scrappier" the quilt. You may also choose to make a more controlled fabric selection by electing to create a two color quilt or by deciding to use the same fabrics in every block.

On the original quilt, after she added a border and had the quilt finished, Mary Schafer signed the name of the top's maker in ink on the quilt. Because a multitude of fabrics appear in the quilt, this textile provides a good study collection of fabrics from the last quarter of the 19th century. Mary's paisley border is a typical print of a fabric available during the time she finished the quilt.

SAWTOOTH QUILT PROJECT

Mary Worrall, piecer and John Putnam, quilter
2001
East Lansing, Ingham County, Michigan
Cotton with cotton/polyester batting
86" x 102"
Photo by Mary Whalen

FLEUR-DE-LIS ALBUM QUILT TOP

Maker unknown
1855
Found in Battle Creek, Calhoun County, Michigan
Cotton
80" x 80"
MSUM 2000:58.1
Photo by Mary Whalen
For more information about this quilt top, see p. 69

Fleur-de-lis Album

◀ Pattern by Beth Donaldson

Finished Quilt Size: $100^1/_2$" x $100^1/_2$"

Finished Block Size: 16"

FABRICS

9 yards cream fabric for background and borders

$4^3/_4$ yards red solid for appliqué, borders, and binding

$3/_8$ yard cuts 7 different red prints for appliqué

9 yards for backing

105" x 105" batting

Fabric marking pencil

Template plastic

The original quilt top does not have borders. We include instructions for the borders on the reproduction quilt on page 69.

CUTTING

Cream:

Cut twenty-five $17^1/_2$" squares for appliqué block backgrounds.

Cut ten $4^1/_2$"-wide strips. Piece end-to-end and cut two $86^1/_2$"-long strips and two $94^1/_2$"-long strips for borders.

Cut fourteen $2^7/_8$"-wide strips, then cut one hundred seventy-two $2^7/_8$" squares for Sawtooth borders.

Cut eight $2^1/_2$" squares for Sawtooth borders.

Red Solid:

Cut nineteen $1^1/_2$"-wide strips. Piece end-to-end and cut two $80^1/_2$"-long strips and two $82^1/_2$"-long strips for inner border. Cut two $98^1/_2$"-long strips and two $100^1/_2$"-long strips for outer border.

Cut fourteen $2^7/_8$"-wide strips, then cut into one hundred seventy two $2^7/_8$" squares for Sawtooth borders.

Use remainder of the red solid and all of the red prints for appliqué designs.

BLOCK ASSEMBLY

Refer to the Appliqué Appendix, page 91.

1. In preparation for Appliqué, finger crease the horizontal, vertical, and diagonal lines of a $17^1/_2$" cream background square.

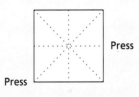

2. Enlarge and trace the fleur-de-lis pattern (page 95) and cut out.

3. Place the template on fabric and mark seam line. Copy the diagonal registration marks onto the seam allowance of the red fabric.

4. Cut around the fleur-de-lis. If using hand appliqué add a $3/_{16}$" seam allowance around the pattern.

5. Sew the 4 seams on the marked lines of the pattern to create one large shape, backstitching at each end of the seam. Sew only between the vertical marks. Press the seam open.

Make 25

6. Align the 4 seams with the horizontal and vertical creases of the background square, and align the diagonal registration lines with the diagonal creases, as shown.

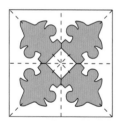

Use the finger pressed creases to center your motif

7. Pin or thread baste the fleur-de-lis to the background.

8. Appliqué using your preferred method. Remove basting, trim the block to $16^1/_2$" x $16^1/_2$". Sign your quilt block. Repeat steps 1-8 to make 25 blocks total.

QUILT ASSEMBLY

1. Arrange the blocks alternating the printed blocks with the solid blocks.

2. Sew the blocks into 5 rows of 5 blocks each. Press the seams of each row in alternate directions. Sew the rows together to complete the top. Press.

3. For inner border, sew the $80^1/_2$"-long red strips to the sides of the quilt, press toward the border. Sew the $82^1/_2$"-long red strips to the top and bottom and press toward the border.

4. To make half-square triangles for Sawtooth borders, layer one dark $2^7/_8$" square and one light $2^7/_8$" square right sides together. Draw a line diagonally from corner to corner. Sew $1/_4$" from both sides of the line. Cut square apart on the drawn line. Press toward the darker fabric. Make 344 $2^1/_2$" half-square triangle units.

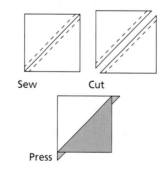

Sew   Cut

Press

5. To make the center Sawtooth for each border, enlarge and trace patterns A, Ar, and B onto template plastic (pages 95). Cut 8 of each pattern. Sew and press, as shown.

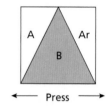

← Press →

6. To make inner Sawtooth borders, sew 4 strips with 20 Sawtooth blocks on either side of a center Sawtooth. Sew 1 of these strips on each side of the quilt top. Press toward the red border.

7. To make the top and bottom inner Sawtooth borders, sew a $2^1/_2$" cream square on each end of 2 Sawtooth strips . Sew these to the top and bottom of the quilt top. Press toward the red border.

8. Sew the two $86^1/_2$" cream strips to the sides of the quilt. Press toward the cream fabric. Sew the two $94^1/_2$" strips to the top and bottom and press toward the cream fabric.

9. To make outer Sawtooth borders, sew 4 strips with 23 Sawtooths on each side of a

FLEUR-DE-LIS ALBUM QUILT PROJECT

Members of the Capitol City Quilt Guild, hand appliquérs; Beth Donaldson, machine piecer and designer; Kari Ruedisale, machine quilter
2001
Lansing, Ingham County, Michigan
Cotton with cotton/polyester filling
100" x 100"
MSUM Teaching Collection
Photo by Mary Whalen

The Capitol City Quilt Guild was started in 1984, the same year as the Michigan Quilt Project inventory was launched.

When the call went out for quilters to hand appliqué the blocks for this quilt on a tight deadline, these members of the guild took up the challenge: Marti Caterino, Pat Clark, Lennie Rathbun, Carol Schon, Norine Antuck, Marie VanTilburg, Beth Donaldson, Kate Edgar, Mary Edgar, Jackie Shulsky, Mary Hausauer, Nancy Johnston, Dorothy Jones, Jan Gagliano, Linda Kuhlman, Mary Hutchins, Phyllis O'Connor, Fran Mort, Carol Seamon, and Jan Quinn.

According to information given to Julie Hacala, the original quilt top was previously acquired in the late 1990s from the estate of 107-year-old Mary Haley, an African-American who lived in Battle Creek, Michigan. However, subsequent research by the MSUM staff reveals that it is more probable that the quilt top was from the estate of Battle Creek resident Olga Haley who died at the age of 104. Her mother, Mary Haley, was born in Kent City, Michigan in 1837 and died in 1864.

center Sawtooth. Sew 1 of these strips on each side of the quilt. Press toward the cream border.

10. To make the top and bottom outer Sawtooth borders, sew a cream $2\frac{1}{2}$" square on each end of 2 Sawtooth strips. Sew these to the top and bottom of the quilt. Press toward the cream border.

11. For outer border, sew the two $98\frac{1}{2}$" red strips to the sides of the quilt, press toward the red border. Sew the

two $100\frac{1}{2}$" strips to the top and bottom and press toward the red border.

QUILTING AND FINISHING

1. Layer top, batting, and backing, then quilt. Echo quilt inside the red fleur-de-lis. Cross-hatch the cream background. Stitch-in-the-ditch on the Sawtooth borders and choose a feather or cable for the inner cream border.

2. To finish, trim to square up the quilt and attach binding.

FANNY'S FAN QUILT

Marguerite Gardner (b. 1878 -1962)
ca. 1930
Grand Rapids, Kent County, Michigan
Cotton with cotton filling
60" x 100"
MSUM 7438.3; Gift of Phyllis Gardner
Photo by KEVA
For more information about this quilt, see p. 73

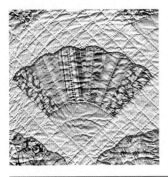

Fanny's Fan

◀ Pattern by Beth Donaldson

Finished Quilt Size: 61³/₄" x 101"

Finished Block Size: 11"

FABRICS

3³/₄ yards total assorted scrap fabrics for 198 fan blades.

Most fan blades in the original museum quilt appear only one time. Base your fabric choices on reproduction fabric lines from the 30s and 40s, then liberally use your fabric stash to create the scrappy look. Have fun!

4 yards cream solid for backgrounds

4 yards pink solid for fan corners, borders, and binding

6 yards for backing

66" x 104" batting

Black #8 pearl cotton

Template plastic

CUTTING

Cream solid:

Cut nine 11¹/₂" strips. Cut strips into twenty-five 11¹/₂" squares.

Cut three 11⁷/₈" strips. Cut strips into eight 11⁷/₈" squares.

Cut one 8⁵/₈" squares.

Pink Solid:

Cut eight 7³/₄"-wide strips. Piece end to end and cut two 85³/₄"-long strips for the side borders and two 61¹/₂"-long strips for the top and bottom borders.

Use the remaining fabric for fan center corners and bias binding.

BLOCK ASSEMBLY

1. Enlarge and trace patterns for the fan blade and the corner onto template plastic on page 95. Cut one corner out of pink solid and 6 blades out of prints for each block.

2. Sew the blades together to create an arc. Sew from the narrow end to the wide end of the blade, stopping ¹/₄" from the wide end of the blade. (This allows you to turn under the edge during appliqué.) Press seams in one direction.

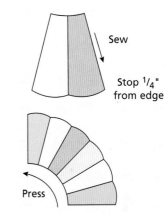

3. Align the arc and the pink fan corner on the background square, as shown. The top edge of the arc is 1³/₄" from the top edge of the square. Use the background to keep the fan square.

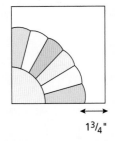

4. Baste the fan arc to the background, leaving room to turn under for appliqué. Baste the pink fan corner to the bottom of the arc only, not the background. The bottom of the arc extends under the pink curve about $1\frac{1}{4}$" to allow for basting and turning under.

5. Using a blanket stitch and #8 black pearl cotton, appliqué the top of the fan to the background, turning under the seam allowance as you stitch. Using a running stitch and #8 black pearl cotton, appliqué the corner to the bottom of the fan blades only, not the background. Trim the backing and bottom of the fan arc to within $\frac{1}{4}$" of the appliqué seams. (See Appliqué Appendix on page 91 for more hints on appliqué.)

6. Repeat to make a total of 25 fan blocks.

7. Using three $11\frac{7}{8}$" background squares, repeat Steps 1-5 above for three more fan blocks. Cut these blocks in half on the horizontal diagonal for use in the top and bottom rows. (You will not use the lower corner of one of the three blocks.)

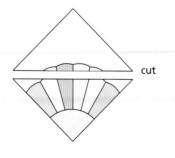

8. Cut five of the $11\frac{7}{8}$" background squares in half on the vertical diagonal to make ten side border triangles. Use three blades and one half fan corner for each side fan. Treat the long side of the background triangle with care to avoid stretching the bias.

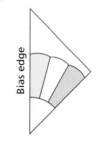

QUILT ASSEMBLY

1. Cut the $8\frac{5}{8}$" square of cream fabric on the diagonal once to make the top corner triangles.

2. Arrange the fan blocks and corner triangles as shown and sew in diagonal rows. Press seam allowances in alternate directions. Sew the rows together and press.

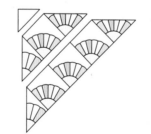

3. Attach the borders to the quilt side borders first and then top and bottom borders. Press toward the borders.

4. Enlarge and transfer the scalloped edge pattern (page 95) to template plastic. Each scallop is half the length of a quilt block. Use the edges of the template and the corners of the blocks to align the scallops. Mark the scallop onto the border. Do not trim until after applying the binding.

QUILTING

1. Layer top, batting, and backing.

2. Quilt in the ditch between each fan blade and stitch through the vertical center of each blade. Echo quilt arcs in the fan corners.

3. Diagonal cross hatch with a 1" grid in the background of each blade. Cross hatch in the corner of each border.

4. Use a simple cable pattern to quilt the border.

5. The outside edge can either be quilted to the edge if you want a plain edge or stitched within the marked scalloped edge.

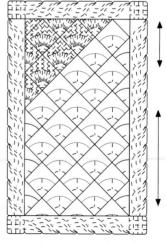

The cable mimics the scalloped edge of the quilt

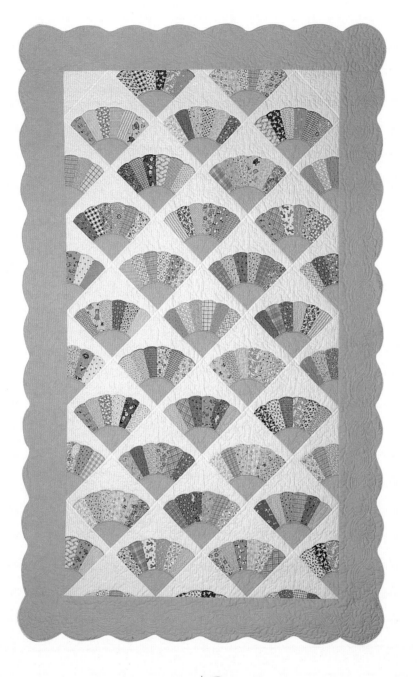

FANNY'S FAN QUILT
PROJECT

Beth Donaldson, designer,
piecer, and appliquér; John
Putnam, machine quilter
2001
Lansing, Ingham County,
Michigan
Cotton with cotton/polyester
filling
62" x 101"
MSUM Teaching Collection
Photo by Mary Whalen

A classic adaptation of a classic
pattern also known as Fanny's
Fan because of the scalloped
edges of the fan blades.
Reproduction fabrics currently
available mixed with fabrics
from Beth's stash make a
brightly-colored quilt with a
cheerful effect. Beth suggests
that "you make sure and
choose some fabrics that you
wouldn't think of as pastel to
keep the palette from washing
out. The original has many
shades of black, brown, and
red that are softened by the
large amount of cream and
pink fabrics used."

Marguerite Moore, the maker
of the original quilt and daughter of Zephiniah and Bernice
Alice Taft Moore, was born in
1878. She graduated from
Hillsdale College with a music
degree and married Charles
Vincent Gardner, a furniture
maker, in 1905. Phyllis, their
only child, believes her mother
learned to quilt from her grandmother and that this is the only
quilt that she made. Phyllis
also remembers some of the
dresses or blouses that were
made of the same fabrics
included in the quilt.

BINDING

1. Make $12^1/_2$ yards of $2^1/_8$"-wide
continuous bias binding from $1^1/_4$"
yards of pink fabric.

2. Place the raw edge of the bias binding along the marked scallop line, right
sides together. Sew $^1/_4$" from the bias
edge, mitering the inner points of each
scallop.

3. Trim the excess fabric and batting
even with the raw edge of binding.

4. Fold the binding to the back and
hand sew in place.

DUCKS IN THE POND QUILT

Mary E. Beardslee Durkee
ca. 1870
Oakland County, Michigan
Cotton
78" x 92"
MSUM 1999:12.6; Quilt from the Durkee-Blakeslee-Quarton-Hoard Collection
Photo by Mary Whalen
For more information about this quilt, see p. 77

Ducks in the Pond

◀ Pattern by Mary Worrall

Finished Quilt Size: 84½" x 96½"

Finished Block Size: 8½"

FABRICS

½ yard each 7 assorted dark fabrics for blocks

½ yard each 7 assorted light fabrics for blocks

4¼ yards dark fabric for setting squares

¾ yard for binding

7¾ yards for backing

89" x 101" batting

Use the cutting instructions for one block if you would like to make each block from different light and dark fabrics.

CUTTING FOR ONE BLOCK

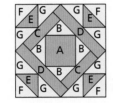

DARK FABRIC:

(A) Cut one 3½" square.

(C) Cut two 1⅜" x 4¾" rectangles.

(D) Cut two 1⅜" x 6½" rectangles.

(E) Cut two 3" squares.

Light Fabric:

(B)(F)(G) Cut eight 3" squares.

Cut 6 of the squares in half diagonally.

CUTTING FOR QUILT

Dark Fabric:

(A) From each of the 7 dark fabrics, cut one 3½"-wide strip. Cut each strip into eight 3½" squares, 56 total.

(C, D) From each of the 7 dark fabrics, cut five 1⅜"-wide strips. Cut the strips into sixteen 1⅜" x 4¾" rectangles and sixteen 1⅜" x 6½" rectangles from each fabric. Cut 112 total of each size.

(E) From each of the 7 dark fabrics, cut two 3"-wide strips. Cut the strips into sixteen 3" squares from each fabric, 112 total.

Light Fabric:

(B)(F)(G) From each of the 7 light fabrics, cut five 3"-wide strips. Cut the strips into sixty-four 3" squares from each fabric. Set 16 squares from each fabric aside to make half-square triangle E/F units. Cut the remaining 48 squares from each fabric in half diagonally for B and G triangles. You will have a total of 672 triangles.

Setting Fabric:

Cut eleven 9"-wide strips. Cut the strips into forty-two 9" squares.

Cut three 13⅜" strips. Cut the strips into seven 13⅜" squares. Cut on both diagonals to make 26 setting triangles.

Cut two 7" squares. Cut the squares in half diagonally to make four corner triangles.

BLOCK ASSEMBLY

To create a scrappier looking quilt, mix and match your darks and lights to create several different block combinations. Refer to the quilt photograph for ideas.

1. To make A/B unit, select one 3½" dark square (A) and four light fabric triangles (B). Sew two of the triangles to opposite sides of the square Press towards dark fabric.

2. Sew the remaining light triangles to the remaining sides of the square. Press towards dark fabric.

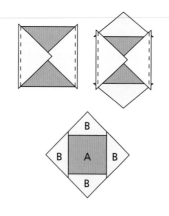

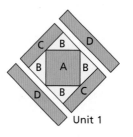

3. Sew 13⅜" x 4¾" rectangle (C) to opposite sides of A/B unit. Press toward C.

4. Sew 13⅜" x 6½" rectangle (D) to the A/B unit's remaining sides. Press toward D. The unit created is unit 1.

5. To make half-square triangle E/F unit, place one 3" light (F) square and one 3" dark (E) square right sides together. Draw a diagonal line on the wrong sides of the fabric. Sew ¼" from both sides of the line. Cut apart on the drawn line. Press toward the dark fabric. Make 4 half-square triangle E/F units for each block.

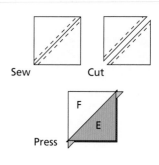

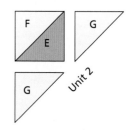

6. Select a half-square triangle E/F unit and 2 light triangles (G). Sew the light triangles to the half-square triangle unit, as shown. Press toward G. The unit created is unit 2. Make 4.

7. Sew two unit 2's to opposite sides of unit 1. Press toward unit 1. Sew the remaining unit 2's to the remaining unit 1 sides. Press toward unit 1. Make 56 blocks.

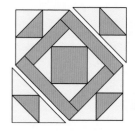

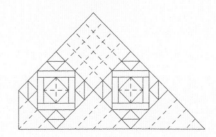

QUILT ASSEMBLY

1. Arrange the pieced blocks, solid blocks, side setting triangles, and corner triangles in a diagonal set, as shown.

2. Sew blocks together into rows. Press toward setting fabric.

3. Sew rows together.

QUILTING AND FINISHING

1. Layer top, batting, and backing, then quilt. The pieced blocks in the original quilt are quilted in the ditch. The setting blocks are quilted in a cross-hatch pattern. The side and corner triangles are quilted diagonally.

2. To finish, trim to square up the quilt and attach binding.

DUCKS IN THE POND QUILT PROJECT

Mary Worrall, designer
Kate Edgar, piecer
Kari Ruedisale, quilter
2001
East Lansing, Ingham County, Michigan
Cotton with cotton/polyester batting
89" x 101"
MSUM Teaching Collection
Photo by Mary Whalen

Kate chose fabrics from her stash of reproduction fabrics to create an even "scrappier" quilt than the pattern suggests.

Donor Betty Quarton Hoard's grandmother, Mary E. Beardslee Durkee, pieced the original version of this quilt with fabrics from the family store. The quilt features madder brown, pink, and purple fabrics in the geometric and abstract prints popular in the 1860-1880 time period. Because the family did not use the quilt, its colors remain bright.

STRING QUILT

Viney Crawford (b. 1912)
1986
Idlewild, Lake County, Michigan
Cotton and polyester
64" x 80"
MSUM 6520.1; Michigan African-American Quilt Collection
Photo by Mary Whalen
For more information about this quilt, see p. 81

String Quilt

◀ Pattern by Mary Worrall

Finished Quilt Size: 61" x 76"

Finished Block Size: 14"

FABRICS

$6\frac{1}{2}$ yards total assorted scrap fabrics for blocks

$3\frac{1}{2}$ yards for foundation fabric (muslin recommended)

1 yard for sashing and first border

$\frac{5}{8}$ yard for binding

$4\frac{1}{2}$ yards for backing

65" x 80" batting

CUTTING

Foundation Fabric:

Cut sixteen $7\frac{1}{2}$"-wide strips. Cut the strips into eighty $7\frac{1}{2}$" squares.

Sashing and Borders:

Cut twenty-one $1\frac{1}{2}$"-wide strips. Piece 13 strips end-to-end. Cut those into five $74\frac{1}{2}$"-long strips for vertical sashing and side borders and two $61\frac{1}{2}$"-long strips for top and bottom borders. From the remaining strips, cut sixteen $14\frac{1}{2}$"-long pieces.

Assorted scrap fabrics:

Cut a large variety of strip sizes, ranging from $1\frac{1}{2}$" to $3\frac{1}{2}$" wide and from 4" to 12" long.

Cut forty $8\frac{1}{4}$" squares, then cut in half diagonally. *(Note: The triangles are oversized to allow for trimming later).*

BLOCK ASSEMBLY

1. Place one $8\frac{1}{4}$" triangle right-side up on a $7\frac{1}{2}$"-square foundation, as shown.

2. Place a piecing strip on top of the triangle (as shown), right sides together. The strip will extend beyond the foundation square. Sew using a $\frac{1}{4}$" seam allowance. Flip piecing strip to right side. Finger press.

3. Add a second strip, as shown. Sew and flip to its right side. Finger press.

4. Continue to add strips to the foundation square in this manner until all of the foundation square is covered. Press unit.

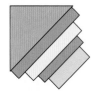

5. Trim the unit to 7^1/$_2$" square. Make 80 units.

6. Arrange the units in clusters of 4. Sew together, as shown, to make 20 blocks.

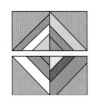

QUILT ASSEMBLY

1. To the lower edges of 16 of the blocks, attach a 14^1/$_2$" x 1^1/$_2$" horizontal sashing strip. Press toward sashing.

2. Sew blocks into columns of 5, as shown. Press toward sashing.

3. Sew 1^1/$_2$" x 74^1/$_2$" vertical sashing strips and side borders to the sides of the columns as shown. Press toward sashing and borders.

4. Add top and bottom borders, as shown. Press toward borders.

QUILTING AND FINISHING

1. Layer and quilt. The original quilt is tied in the centers of the blocks and in the sashing.

2. To finish, trim to square up quilt and attach border.

STRING QUILT PROJECT

Mary Worrall, designer and piecer; John Putnam, quilter
2000-2001
East Lansing, Ingham County, Michigan
Cotton with cotton/polyester batting
61" x 76"
MSUM Teaching Collection
Photo by Mary Whalen

By choosing a darker sashing, this quilt takes on an entirely new look, which sets off the brightly-colored fabrics within.

Within the African-American community, Nine-Patch and Strip pattern quilts done in the String technique are most often cited by quilters as the first ones they learned and continue to prefer. Viney Crawford, of Idlewild, made this String quilt especially for the Michigan State University Museum in honor of the Yates Township Senior Center in Idlewild. Idlewild, located in a rural area of Michigan's lower peninsula, was developed in 1912 as a resort for the growing numbers of middle-class African-Americans. In its heyday, the resort hosted a who's who list of African-Americans prominent in all walks of life and was a destination for many of some of the nation's most notable performers. An African-American Quilt Discovery Day was held in Idlewild in July, 1986.

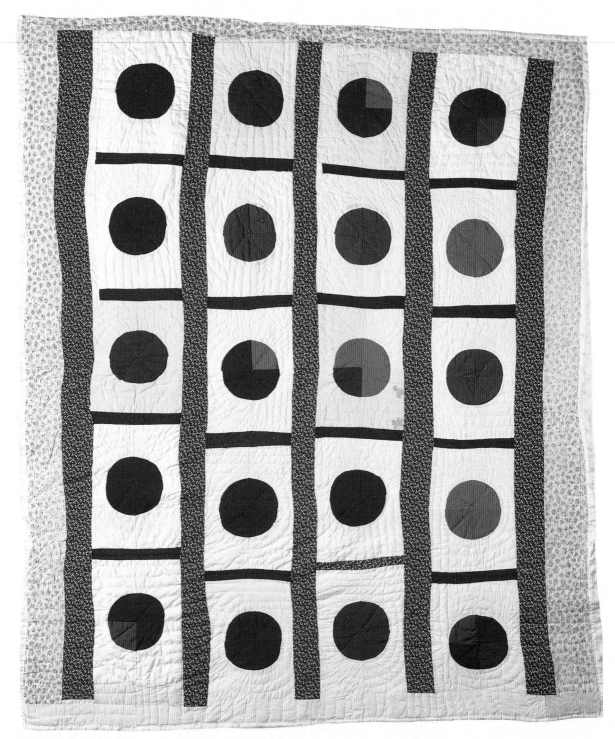

STOVE EYE QUILT

Mary Atkins
1987
Kalamazoo, Kalamazoo County, Michigan
Cotton and cotton blends with cotton flannel filling
77" x 86"
MSUM Accession 7132.1; Michigan African-American Quilt Collection
Photo by Mary Whalen
For more information about this quilt, see p. 85

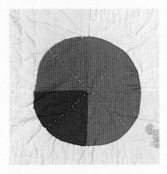

Stove Eye Quilt

◀ Pattern by Mary Worrall

Finished Quilt Size: $73^1/_2$" x $94^1/_2$"

Finished Block Size: 12" x 16"

FABRIC

$1^1/_2$ yards assorted reds and oranges for the circle segments

4 yards cream for background

$^1/_2$ yard red for solid horizontal sashing

$1^1/_3$ yards red print for vertical sashing

$1^1/_4$ yards light print for borders

$^2/_3$ yard for binding

6 yards for backing

78" x 99" batting

Template plastic

CUTTING

Circle Fabric:

Enlarge Pattern A on page 94 and trace onto template plastic. Cut 80 quarter circles. Transfer the center registration marks onto the fabric.

Background:

Cut twenty $6^1/_2$"-wide strips.

Enlarge Pattern B on page 94 and trace onto template plastic. Cut 40 background pieces. Turn template upside down and cut 40 more pieces. Transfer the center registration marks.

Horizontal Sashing:

Cut six $2^1/_2$"-wide strips, then cut into sixteen $12^1/_2$" pieces.

Vertical Sashing:

Cut twelve $3^1/_2$"-wide strips. Piece end-to-end and cut five $88^1/_2$"-long strips.

Side Borders:

Cut five $5^1/_2$"-wide strips. Piece end-to-end and cut two $88^1/_2$"-long strips.

Top and Bottom Borders:

Cut four $3^1/_2$"-wide strips. Piece end-to-end and cut two $73^1/_2$"-long strips.

BLOCK ASSEMBLY

1. Place background on top of a circle piece, right sides together. Match the center registration marks.

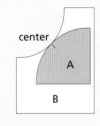

2. Pin and sew, easing the two pieces together, clipping where necessary. Press toward circle piece A.

3. Group the pieced sections into sets of 4; sew to form blocks, as shown. In the original quilt, the circle sections are not perfectly matched. Press. Make 20 blocks total.

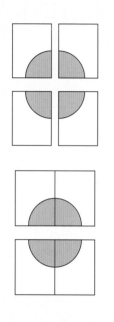

QUILT ASSEMBLY

1. Sew blocks and horizontal sashing pieces together, as shown. Press toward sashing. Make 4 sets of 5 blocks each.

2. Sew the vertical sashing to the sides of the block sets. Press toward sashing.

3. Sew the side borders to the quilt top, as shown. Press toward borders.

4. Sew the top and bottom borders to the quilt top. Press toward borders.

QUILTING AND FINISHING

1. Layer and quilt. See illustration for quilting suggestions.

2. To finish, trim to square up quilt and attach binding.

Quilting design

STOVE EYE QUILT PROJECT

Mary Worrall, designer and piecer; Kari Ruedisale, quilter
2001
East Lansing, Ingham County, Michigan
Cotton with cotton/polyester batting
74" x 94"
MSUM Teaching Collection
Photo by Mary Whalen

The reproduction was made in a similar palette to the original. To create a greater texture within the quilt top, however, batiks, rather than solids, were used.

Mary Atkins grew up in rural Arkansas and was about eight years old when she learned to quilt from her mother who made quilts for family use. According to Atkins, her mother taught her and her sisters to quilt in order to keep them out of mischief after they finished school or after doing their chores on the family farm. "There was no playing after work, but I'd sit down on a stool and begin piecing." Mary Atkins even found inspiration for this design when she saw a bedcovering in a television advertisement for waterbeds. It is unknown why the quilter titled this "Stove Eye."

FOUR-PATCH VARIATION QUILT

Elizabeth Samantha Fowler Weatherbee
(b.1840 - death date unknown), piecer; quilter unknown
Top dates to 1903, quilted 1969
Provenance unknown
Cotton
68" x 78"
MSUM 6581.2; Gift of Florence Vogt
Photo by KEVA
For more information about this quilt, see p. 90

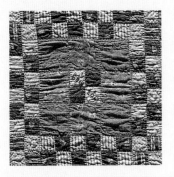

Four-Patch Variation

◄ Pattern by Mary Worrall

Finished Quilt Size: 76" x 84"

Finished Block Size: 4"

FABRICS

Center Four-Patch block:

Scrap each of 1 light and 1 dark

Rows B & C: $1/4$ yard each of 2 lights and 2 darks

Rows D & E: $1/3$ yard each of 2 lights and 2 darks

Rows F & G: $1/2$ yard each of 2 lights and 2 darks

Rows I & J: $2/3$ yard each of 1 light and 1 dark

Row K: $1/2$ yard each of 1 light and 1 dark

$2/3$ yard for binding

5 yards for backing

80" x 88" batting

CUTTING

Center Four-Patch Block:

Cut two $2^1/_2$" squares from each of 2 light and 2 dark fabrics.

Row B:

Cut four $4^1/_2$" squares from each of 2 light and 2 dark fabrics.

Row C:

Cut two $2^1/_2$"-wide strips from each of 1 light and 1 dark fabric.

Row D:

Cut two $4^1/_2$"-wide strips from each of 1 light and 1 dark fabric. Cut the strips into twelve $4^1/_2$" squares each.

Row E:

Cut four $2^1/_2$"-wide strips from each of 1 light and 1 dark fabric.

Row F:

Cut three $4^1/_2$" wide strips from each of 1 light and 1 dark fabric. Cut strips into twenty $4^1/_2$" squares each.

Row G:

Cut six $2^1/_2$"-wide strips from each of 1 light and 1 dark fabric.

Row H:

Cut three $4^1/_2$"-wide strips from each of 1 light and 1 dark fabric. Cut strips into twenty-eight $4^1/_2$" squares each.

Row I:

Cut eight $2^1/_2$"-wide strips from each of 1 light and 1 dark fabric.

Row J:

Cut five $4^1/_2$"-wide strips from each of 1 light and 1 dark fabric. Cut into thirty-six $4^1/_2$" squares each.

Row K:

Cut five $2^1/_2$"-wide strips from each of 1 light and 1 dark fabric, or use the leftover strips from the other rows.

BLOCK ASSEMBLY

To make the Four-Patch blocks:

Sew $2^{1}/_{2}$"-wide light and dark strips together in pairs. Press seam toward the dark strip. Cut strips into $2^{1}/_{2}$" segments. Sew units together into a Four-Patch block, as shown.

$2^{1}/_{2}$" $2^{1}/_{2}$"

Four-Patch

QUILT ASSEMBLY

Assemble the quilt one row at a time, working from the center of the quilt to the edges (round-robin). Press seams in each strip in alternating directions. When adding each row to the quilt top, press seams toward the solid block strips.

Center Four-Patch:

Make one Four-Patch block.

Row B:

Sew a dark $4^{1}/_{2}$" square to both sides of the center Four-Patch. Press as arrows indicate.

Sew a light $4^{1}/_{2}$" square to either side of the remaining dark squares. Press as arrows indicate.

Attach to the top and bottom of the center Four-Patch.

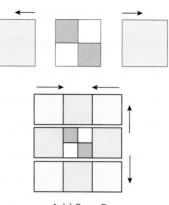

Add Row B

Row C:

Make 16 Four-Patch blocks. Sew 2 sets of 3 blocks and add to the sides of the center unit. Press. Sew 2 sets of 5 blocks, and add to the top and bottom of the center unit. Press.

Add Row C

Row D:

Sew 2 sets of five $4^{1}/_{2}$" squares, alternating light and dark. Add to sides of the center unit. Press.

Sew 2 sets with seven $4^{1}/_{2}$" squares, alternating light and dark. Add to the top and bottom of the center unit. Press.

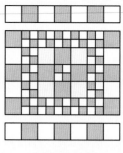

Add Row D

Row E:

Make 32 Four-Patch blocks. Sew 2 sets of 7 blocks and add to the sides of the center unit. Press.

Sew 2 sets of nine blocks and add to the top and bottom of the center unit. Press.

Add Row E

Row F:

Sew 2 sets of nine $4^{1}/_{2}$" squares, alternating dark and light. Add to the sides of the center unit. Press.

Sew 2 sets of eleven $4^{1}/_{2}$" squares, alternating dark and light. Add to the top and bottom of the center unit. Press.

Row G:

Make 48 Four-Patch blocks. Sew two sets of 11 blocks and

add to the sides of the center unit. Press.

Sew 2 sets of 13 blocks and add to the top and bottom of the center unit. Press.

Row H:

Sew 2 sets of thirteen $4^1/_2$" squares, alternating dark and light. Add to the sides of the center unit. Press.

Sew 2 sets of fifteen $4^1/_2$" squares, alternating dark and light. Add to the top and bottom of the center unit. Press.

Row I:

Make 64 Four-Patch blocks. Sew 2 sets of 15 blocks and add to the sides of the center unit. Press.

Sew 2 sets of 17 blocks and add to the top and bottom of the center unit. Press.

Row J:

Sew 2 sets of seventeen $4^1/_2$" squares, alternating dark and light. Add to the sides of the center unit. Press.

Sew 2 sets of nineteen $4^1/_2$" squares, alternating dark and light. Add to the top and bottom of the center unit. Press.

Row K:

Use remaining fabric pieces from cut strips (rows D to J) to make 38 Four-Patch blocks. Sew 2 sets of 19 blocks and add only to the top and bottom of the quilt. Press.

QUILTING AND FINISHING

1. Layer top, batting, and backing; quilt. The original quilt is stitched-in-the-ditch.

2. To finish, trim to square up the quilt and attach binding.

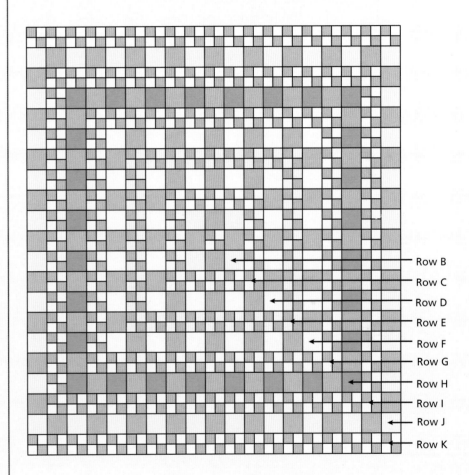

Row B
Row C
Row D
Row E
Row F
Row G
Row H
Row I
Row J
Row K

With the many reproduction fabrics available, creating a reproduction of the Four-Patch Variation was easy. Changing to brightly-colored fabrics would give the quilt a much different look. The simple shapes make this a great quilt for beginners.

This quilt's fabrics—shirtings in a palette of wine red, navy, gray-blue, and blacks—are very typical of their era. Simple patterns such as this Four-Patch became very popular at the end of the 19th century. The original quilt top was made by Elizabeth to commemorate the birth of her grandson, Benjamin E. Weatherbee. The top was later finished by an unidentified quilter who embroidered "1903/1969" in its center. Florence Vogt received the quilt in the mid-70s from her cousin and his wife because they knew she loved quilts and they had no children to inherit it.

Four-Patch Variation Quilt Project

Mary Worrall and Barbara Worrall, piecers; Kari Ruedisale, quilter
2000-2001
East Lansing and Howell, Ingham and Livingston Counties, Michigan
Cotton with cotton/polyester batting
76" x 84"
MSUM Teaching Collection
Photo by Mary Whalen

Appliqué Appendix

APPLIQUÉ

There are many ways to appliqué and clever quilters are inventing new ways all the time. All the patterns given are suitable for both hand and machine methods. Feel free to use your favorite method on any patterns supplied. The quilts we chose to pattern all used different techniques. Don't worry if all your curves aren't smooth, your stitches aren't perfect or your appliqués aren't perfectly aligned. Neither are the featured quilts. Remember to keep it fun, you'll then be historically correct!

Rather than divide the methods into hand or machine, we describe steps that you can mix-and-match.

Transferring the Pattern

All the patterns for appliqué (with the exception of the fans) are given with no seam allowance. You will need to add a $^3/_{16}$" seam allowance around each pattern. Trace the pattern without seam allowance onto freezer paper to create the template. Make sure to include any registration marks that are included in the pattern. Carefully cut out the template. With a hot iron, press the freezer paper onto the right side of your fabric (for patterns that will be used many, many times, use template plastic and trace around the template rather than pressing it onto the fabric). Use a marking pencil and draw around the template. Transfer any registration marks onto the fabric into the seam allowance. Remove the paper. By eye, cut the fabric out including a $^3/_{16}$" seam allowance.

Turning Under the Seam Allowance

If you are choosing to hand appliqué, you may needle turn under the seam allowance as you sew. Make sure you turn just beyond the drawn line, so the drawn line ends up in the seam allowance. You may also turn and baste the seam allowance before you appliqué. This requires thread or glue basting the seam allowance. Again you want to make sure you turn just beyond the drawn line. This is usually done if you are choosing to machine appliqué. With either method, smooth curves are achieved when the seam allowance is evenly distributed in the process.

Stitching Choices

The different quilts in the projects have used different stitching styles. After centering and layering your appliqués either thread or pin baste them to the background fabric. *Rose in the Window* was done with needle-turn hand appliqué. The reproduction *Fanny's Fan* was done using multi-colored, #8 pearl cotton with blanket stitches in the fan blades and black #8 pearl cotton in a running stitch in the fan corners. Both stitches were done by hand and machine.

For the *Star of Bethlehem*, machine appliqué was used in the project. In the museum version hand appliqué was used. The *Fleur-de-lis Album* uses needle turn hand appliqué.

NEEDLE TURN APPLIQUÉ

Bring the needle up through the fold, catching a few threads of the fabric. Clip any inner corners and use extra stitches to help with sharp points.

BUTTONHOLE STITCH, BY HAND

Bring the needle up through the appliqué edge, with the tip over the working thread. Pull the stitch into place until the thread is slightly taut. Hold the working thread with your thumb and take another stitch. Repeat the process. Keeping the stitches even.

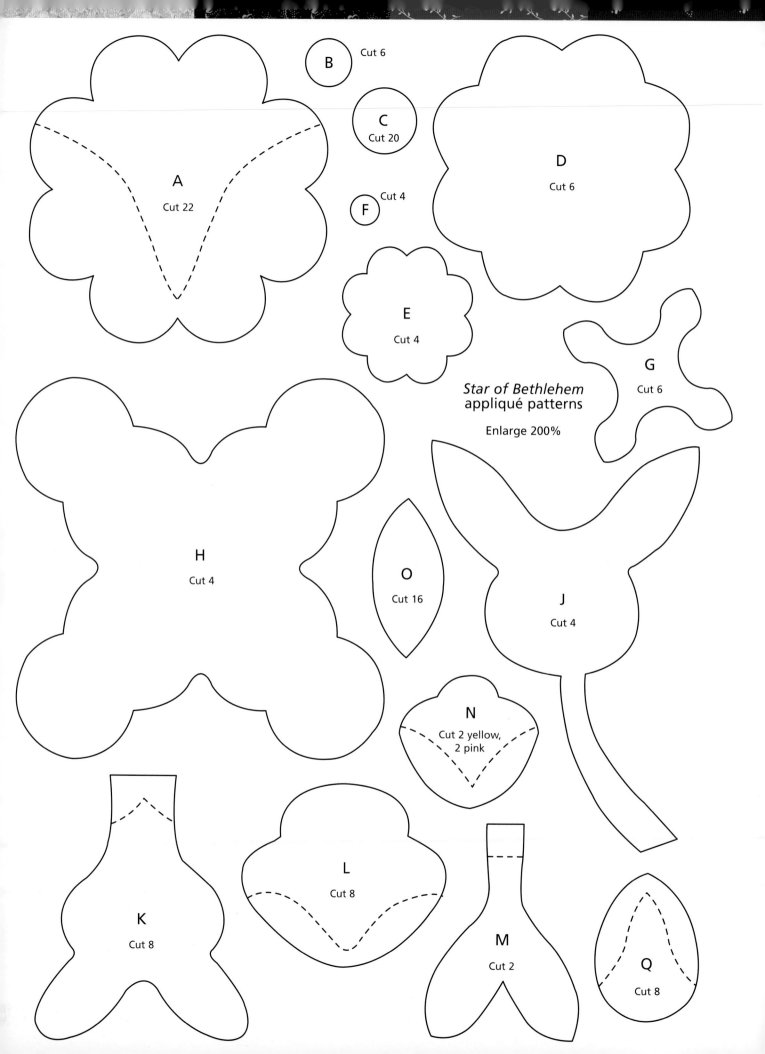

B
Cut 6

C
Cut 20

A
Cut 22

D
Cut 6

F
Cut 4

E
Cut 4

Star of Bethlehem
appliqué patterns

Enlarge 200%

G
Cut 6

H
Cut 4

O
Cut 16

J
Cut 4

N
Cut 2 yellow,
2 pink

K
Cut 8

L
Cut 8

M
Cut 2

Q
Cut 8

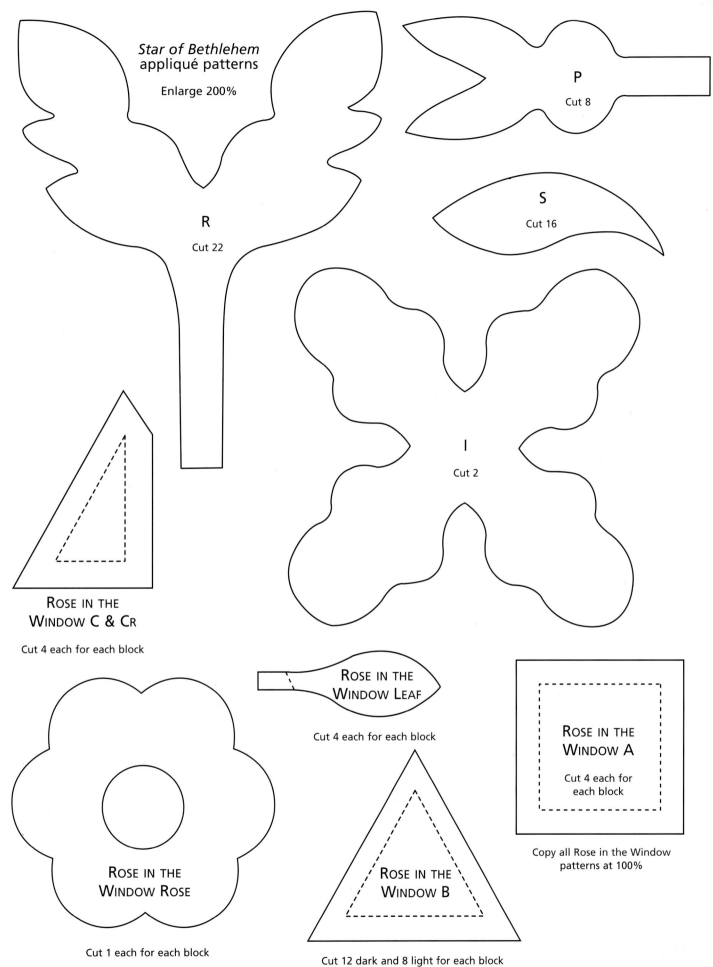

Star of Bethlehem
appliqué patterns

Enlarge 200%

P
Cut 8

S
Cut 16

R
Cut 22

I
Cut 2

ROSE IN THE
WINDOW C & Cʀ

Cut 4 each for each block

ROSE IN THE
WINDOW LEAF

Cut 4 each for each block

ROSE IN THE
WINDOW A

Cut 4 each for
each block

Copy all Rose in the Window
patterns at 100%

ROSE IN THE
WINDOW ROSE

Cut 1 each for each block

ROSE IN THE
WINDOW B

Cut 12 dark and 8 light for each block

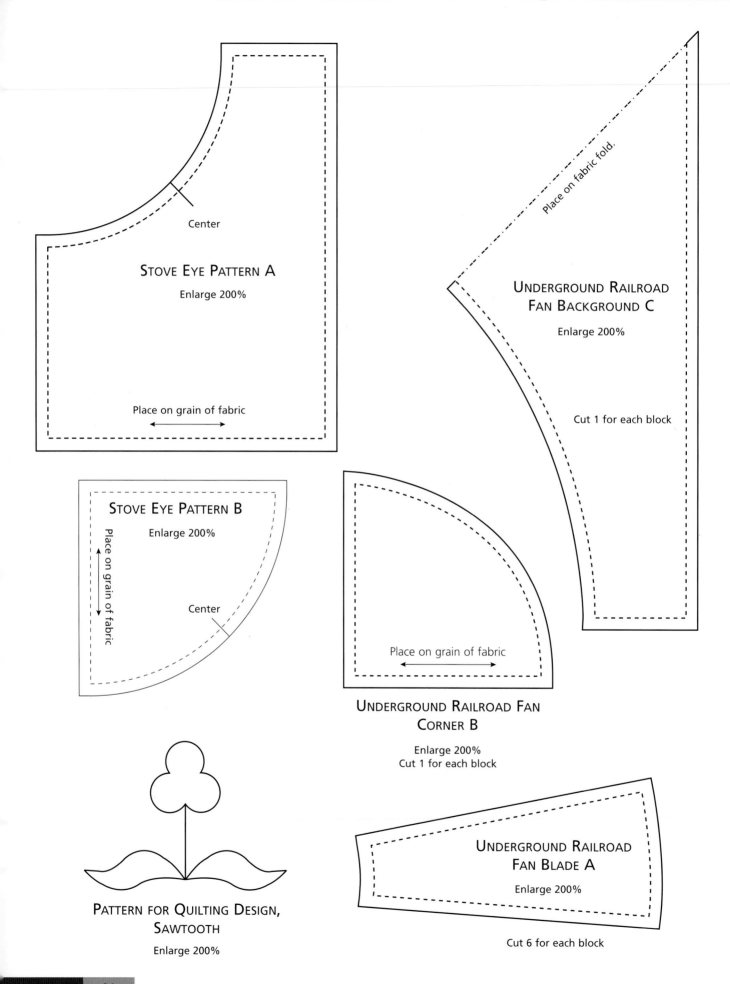

STOVE EYE PATTERN A

Enlarge 200%

Center

Place on grain of fabric

**UNDERGROUND RAILROAD
FAN BACKGROUND C**

Enlarge 200%

Place on fabric fold.

Cut 1 for each block

STOVE EYE PATTERN B

Enlarge 200%

Place on grain of fabric

Center

**UNDERGROUND RAILROAD FAN
CORNER B**

Enlarge 200%
Cut 1 for each block

Place on grain of fabric

**PATTERN FOR QUILTING DESIGN,
SAWTOOTH**

Enlarge 200%

**UNDERGROUND RAILROAD
FAN BLADE A**

Enlarge 200%

Cut 6 for each block

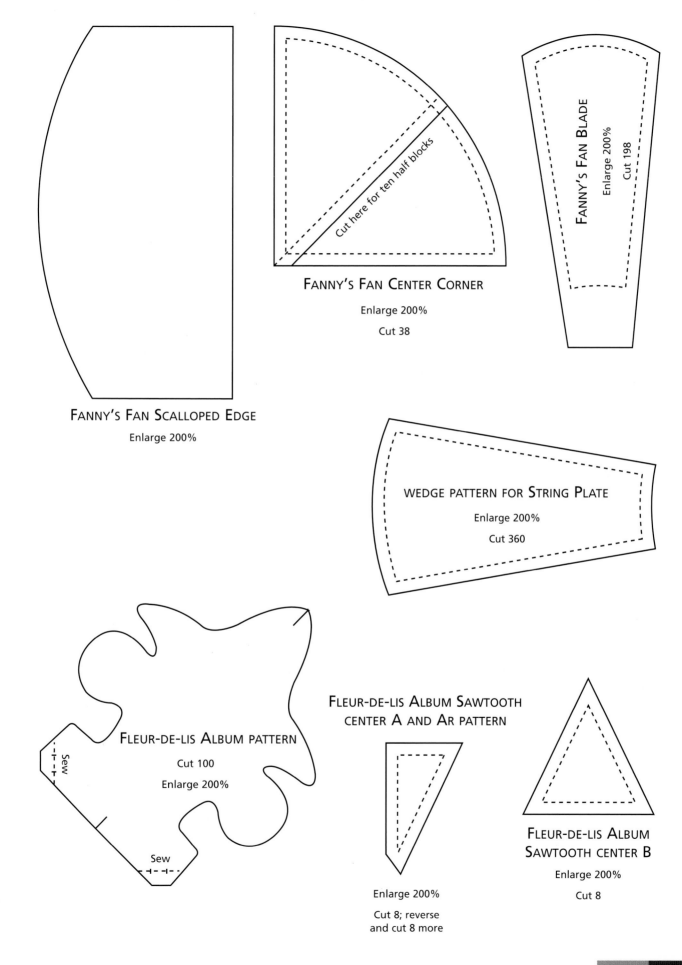

FANNY'S FAN CENTER CORNER

Enlarge 200%

Cut 38

Cut here for ten half blocks

FANNY'S FAN BLADE

Enlarge 200%

Cut 198

FANNY'S FAN SCALLOPED EDGE

Enlarge 200%

WEDGE PATTERN FOR STRING PLATE

Enlarge 200%

Cut 360

FLEUR-DE-LIS ALBUM pattern

Cut 100

Enlarge 200%

Sew

Sew

FLEUR-DE-LIS ALBUM SAWTOOTH
CENTER A AND AR PATTERN

Enlarge 200%

Cut 8; reverse
and cut 8 more

FLEUR-DE-LIS ALBUM
SAWTOOTH CENTER B

Enlarge 200%

Cut 8

Bibliography

General references

Bassett, Lynne Z. and Jack Larkin, *Northern Comfort New England's Early Quilts 1780 – 1850*, Rutledge Hill Press, Nashville Tennessee, 1998, p. 32.]

Bishop, Kathleen. "Quiltmakers of Liberia," pp. 47-48 in TOPICS (Summer 1989); reprinted in *Women of Color Quilt Network Newsletter*, Fall 1990.

Brackman, Barbara, *Clues in the Calico A Guide to Identifying and Dating Antique Quilts*. McLean, Virginia: EPM Publications, Inc., 1989.

Brackman, Barbara, "Quilts at Chicago's World Fairs," pp. 63-76 in *Uncoverings* 1981, Volume 2 of the Research Papers of the American Quilt Study Group.

Conroy, Mary. *300 Years of Canada's Quilts*. Toronto, Ontario: Griffin House, 1976.

Dewhurst, C. Kurt, Yvonne Lockwood, and Marsha MacDowell. *Michigan: Whose Story? A Celebration of the State's Traditions*. East Lansing, Michigan: Michigan State University Museum, 1985.

Finley, Ruth E. *Old Patchwork Quilts and the Women Who Made Them*. McLean, Virginia: EPM Publications, 1992 (originally published in 1929), pp. 62-63.

Gangyi, Dai and Guo Youmin, *Shaanxi Folk Arts*, Kow Loon, Hong Kong: Sinminchu Publishing Company, 1988.

Hunt, Gail. *Quilt Works Across Canada: Eleven Contemporary Workshops*. North Vancouver, Canada: Pacific Quiltworks, Ltd., 1996.

Kelley, Helen. *Scarlet Ribbons: American Indian Technique for Today's Quilters*. Paducah, Kentucky: American Quilter's Society, 1987.

MacDowell, Marsha. *Stories in Thread: Hmong Pictorial Embroidery*. East Lansing: Michigan State University Museum, 1989.

MacDowell, Marsha and C. Kurt Dewhurst, eds. *Michigan-Hmong Arts*. East Lansing: Michigan State University Museum, 1983.

MacDowell, Marsha and C. Kurt Dewhurst, eds. *To Honor and Comfort: Native Quilting Traditions*. Santa Fe, New Mexico: Museum of New Mexico Press in collaboration with Michigan State University Museum, 1997.

MacDowell, Marsha and Margaret Wood. "Sewing it Together: Native American and Hawaiian Quilting Traditions," in Akwe:Kon Journal, Vol. XI, Nos. 3 & 4, special issue, *Native American Expressive Culture* published in collaboration with the National Museum of the American Indian.

MacDowell, Marsha and Janice Reed, eds. *Sisters of the Great Lakes: Art of American Indian Women*. East Lansing, Michigan: Michigan State University Museum in collaboration with the Nokomis American Indian Cultural Learning Center, 1995.

Pilgrim, Paul D. and Gerald E. Roy. *Gatherings: America's Quilt Heritage*. Paducah, Kentucky: American Quilter's Society, 1995.

Safford, Carleton L. and Robert Bishop. *America's Quilts and Coverlets*. New York: Weathervane Books, 1974.

Schmahmann, Brenda. "A History of the Weya Appliqué Project," pp. 40 - in Brenda Schmahmann, ed. *Material Matters*, Johannesburg, South Africa: Witwatersrand University Press, 2000.

Tristain, Eileen Jahnke. *Dating Fabrics: A Color Guide 1800-1960*. Paducah, Kentucky: American Quilter's Society, 1998.

Vaz, Kim Marie. *The Woman with the Artistic Brush: A Life History of Yoruba Black Artist Nike Davies*. Armonk, New York: M. E. Sharpe, 1995.

Webster's II New Riverside Dictionary. New York: Houghton Mifflin Company, 1996.

For more information write for a free catalog:

C&T Publishing, Inc.
P.O. Box 1456
Lafayette, CA 94549
(800) 284-1114
e-mail: ctinfo@ctpub.com
website: www.ctpub.com